PRIDE'S CONSEQUENCES

AND

HUMILITY'S BLESSINGS

By

Luis Ruiz, Ph.D.

DEDICATION

I want to give all the glory to the Lord Jesus Christ. Any spiritual growth, any true joy, any earthly accomplishment are only possible through His reconciliatory ministry. I also thank God for my wife, children and church family whose prayers, encouragement and guidance have been immeasurable. My prayer is that this work can bring those that are "searching for something" to a saving knowledge of Christ and that those already "born-again" grow in their Christian walk.

> *"Be thou exalted, O God, above the heavens: and thy glory above all the earth;" (Ps 108:5)*

PREFACE

An Excellent Book written by my dear friend, Dr. Luis Ruiz. I have read it over and over, and the more I read it, the more I enjoy it and glean from it.

Deep in the soul of man, rooted in the deepest of his heart, is the sin of pride.

Dr. Luis Ruiz thoughtfully deals with the issue of pride, using sensitivity and wisdom.

This book will help you identify pride, its evil works and its consequences. It will instruct you on how to bring pride into submission using Scripture.

It does not only present the dangers of an unbridled pride, but it also presents its antidote, HUMILITY, and the blessedness of it.

Within each chapter, you will find truth filled Scriptures and wise reflections that will move you to search within the depths of your heart.

Human beings should be the least proud, yet are the most prone to arrogance.

"A proud heart... is sin" Pro. 21:4

His plowing, his labor, is for pride and not for the glory of God. The whole husbandry of the proud is sin.

I know this book will help you, and will bless you as it has blessed me.

"The sin of pride turned Luzbel into Lucifer.
The Light bearer was sunk into darkness.
Pride was the first sin in the Garden of Eden,
Pride destroyed the life and kingdom of the first King of Israel.
Pride will take many souls to Hell, more than any other sin."[1]

Dr. Humberto Gómez, D.D., Translator
Reina Valera Gómez Spanish Translation
September, 2012

---

[1] Poem by Dr. Humberto Gómez.

I have known Dr. Luis Ruiz for several years. Being residents of the same state, we have had several opportunities to meet in person as well as speak over the phone. He and his family have visited our church. He also attended the 2011 Dean Burgon Society meeting. I have even been used by the Lord to recommend the university where he eventually attained his doctorate.

I have looked through the entire book. It is thorough. It is Biblical. It is practical. It will reach into the heart and soul of its readers. It is intense. It is insightful. I believe it will meet the spiritual needs of its readers. The book is enriched by helpful paragraph headings which make it easy for the reader to follow his ideas. Dr. Ruiz is also to be commended for his use of the King James Bible for all the references throughout the work.

The book has 21 chapters, the first 10 deal with the problem of sinful pride. The last 11 chapters explain the solution of godly humility. The problem of pride is illustrated by the use of Scripture and by many illustrations from both the Bible and from everyday life. The solution to the sin of pride is the Biblical application of godly humility.

The need for this book for Bible-believing Christians is especially evident in view of the current pompous, boastful, sinful pride of many ministers, evangelists, Christian leaders, and lay people. There is a desperate need in churches, schools, homes, and hearts for a total forsaking of all personal pride, and a total reception and adoption of true Biblical humility.

I believe the proper use and application of this book will bring Biblical answers to both the problem of sinful pride and the solution of godly humility.

Pastor D A Waite, Th.D., Ph.D.
Bible For Today Baptist Church,
Collingswood, New Jersey
September, 2012

TABLE OF CONTENTS

14

INTRODUCTION

The Reasons For This Book

The Holy Spirit led me to select the topic of "Pride's Consequences and Humility's Blessings" for several reasons. First, it was an area where the Lord revealed my need for immediate growth. It was only after delving into the many Scripture verses that the matter's urgent realization became clear. Not surprisingly, I had never done an exhaustive study on this particular Biblical theme. Most importantly, the Lord had placed in my heart a desire to become a more useful vessel for God. As such, my prayer and supplication is that I continue to grow in Christ and be used more commendably in evangelism and discipleship.

Furthermore, I have been mightily blessed as I have carefully studied many Scriptures and the writings of Godly men. What became evident early on was how pride is easy and natural to the flesh while humility is often difficult and can really only be acquired by supernatural means. This study has yielded immediate fruit with respect to how certain life challenges are viewed and approached. Most telling is the realization of how much one needs to "die daily" in order to purge pride's stealth and insidious character. Immature believers may have intellectual knowledge of "dying-to-self" but often do not start putting it into practice until much later in their walk with Jesus Christ. This should not really surprise mature saints since this is what the Bible describes as *the process of sanctification*.

> *Wherefore, my beloved, as ye have always obeyed, not as in my presence only, but now much more in my absence, work out your own salvation with fear and trembling. (Phil. 2:12)*

When Salvation Produces "Good Deeds"

The main observation on the Philippians passage above is that true salvation needs to be revered and nurtured daily through obedience, prayer, Bible reading, and fellowship with other believers. The Bible is resoundingly emphatic that one can never do enough "good" to earn salvation. It can only be received through repentance and heart belief in Jesus Christ. Only then can one "work out" their salvation on a daily basis. This is when good deeds come to fruition.

A great part of this "working out" comes from identifying pride's pervasiveness and earnestly restraining it in our everyday existence. Therefore, I truly hope that anyone who reads this faithful attempt at presenting such a critical aspect of the Christian walk will be blessed and come to similar convictions about the pride in their lives:

> "That demon of pride was born with us, and it will not die one hour before us."[2]

---

[2] Charles Haddon Spurgeon.
http://www.Spurgeon.us/mind_and_heart/quotes/p4.htm#pride (accessed October 3, 2011).

CHAPTER 1

THE REAL BEGINNINGS OF PRIDE

After the heavens and earth were formed...after the creation of light, firmament, land, sun, moon, stars, fowl and beast...even after the creation of man, there was with God another being full of wisdom, full of beauty and perfect in his ways. This was so from the moment he was created by God. He was covered in every precious stone and walked the Holy Mountain of God. Musical dominion was his from the very moment he was fashioned. All was given to him well beyond his necessities. One could even say that he was a "prince" or "king" of some domain. What more could anyone want?

Suddenly, the account shifts as iniquity and sin were found in him. It was disclosed that all he was given was not enough to satisfy his desires. Building an unholy alliance, he was found trading and trafficking and was soon filled with violence. In his heart, he wanted to exalt his given principality above the stars of God and place it on the mount of the congregation. There he could ascend into the heights of the clouds and be like the most High God. His refusal to have anyone above him was fully divulged.

The account intensely shifts again as the Holy and Just Creator acts to reveal and execute the punishment of this being's treachery and iniquity. He would first be unceremoniously cast out of the mountain of God (Heaven) down to the Earth. Once on Earth, he would then weaken the nations, hold court with kings and be a terror for all of mankind. Eventually he would be devoured and destroyed. Several thousands of years after rebelling, his ultimate consequence is to be cast a second time...this time into the eternal lake of fire. His pomp would be brought down to the grave! One cannot escape the irony of him walking "in the midst of the stones of fire" prior to his first expulsion only to be thrown into a similar environment after his second and final expulsion. (Ezek. 28:11-19, Isa. 14:11-14.)

The First Record of Rebellion and Sin

Just presented is the Bible's first record of rebellion and sin against God. The seed that triggered this insurgence was none other than pride. The created being is of course the "Anointed Cherub" or "Lucifer," whose name would be eventually changed to Satan or Devil.

The Five "I Will" Statements of Lucifer

Shedding further light on Satan's rebellion, Isaiah chapter 14 outlines the five "I will" statements of Lucifer. The passage reads:

> *For thou hast said in thine heart, I will ascend into heaven, I will exalt my throne above the stars of God: I will sit also upon the mount of the congregation, in the sides of the north: I will ascend above the heights of the clouds; I will be like the most High. (vs.13-14)*

Lucifer desired above all a position of prominence; to be exalted above all. He was not satisfied with all that was given to him. Being possibly number two was not sufficient. This is ironic because nothing that he had in heaven was earned. It was all given to him by his Creator! However, he began comparing his position to that of God. Once it became comparative, then it took the sin form of covetousness.

The Nature of Pride

The sin of pride is frequently masked as people only see the more visible avarice and covetousness. Too often, this camouflaging with other sins makes pride's detection tremendously difficult, even for born-again saints. But make no mistake, pride is there as the dreadful foundation.

Pride does not take pleasure in having something; it typically takes pleasure in having something that someone else does not have. As expected, the Words of God provide very vivid descriptions of pride's comparative nature. In Ezekiel 16:56, Judah's collective pride never allowed it to think itself as bad as Sodom. Likewise, in Matthew 7:3-5, our Lord and Savior describes how many are often concerned with the "*small*" sins of others while ignoring their own often "*larger*" sins. The narrative testifies:

> *And why beholdest thou the mote that is in thy brother's eye, but considerest not the beam that is in thine own eye? Or how wilt thou say to thy brother, Let me pull out the mote out of thine eye; and, behold, a beam is in thine own eye? Thou hypocrite, first cast out the beam out of thine own eye; and then shalt thou see clearly to cast out the mote out of thy brother's eye.*

Another well-known verse on this matter is found in Luke 18:11. Jesus Christ, in one of His parables, utters,

> *"The Pharisee stood and prayed thus with himself, God, I thank thee, that I am not as other men are, extortioners, unjust, adulterers, or even as this publican."*

The sin of pride is uncovered yet again as the Pharisee is "praying" comparatively. His heart treacherously believes that he is holier than the common everyday sinner. Not often articulated is the fact that the same evil that drives Satan's pride is also the central theme of all three passages above. An all-important question to be asked is, "How frequently does this happen to today's believer?" The Christian should take heed of this question and admit that sinful pride can even be rooted in piety and worship to God. A Christian author cites,

> "Pride is one of Satan's chief weapons. If he can get a pastor proud of his preaching, a Sunday school teacher proud of his class's growth or a church officer proud of his experience and leadership, then Satan has a foothold from which to launch his attack."[3]

Many other displays and manifestations of pride will be examined later in the book.

---

[3] Warren Wiersbe, <u>The Strategy of Satan</u> (Carol Stream, IL: Tyndale House Publishers, 1979), 57.

Pride's Origin

Returning to the account of Satan, quite possibly the most essential aspect of Lucifer's "I will" statements was that they originated from his heart. The Bible is clear that Satan's heart was lifted-up (Ezek. 28:17) and that he spoke from his heart (Isa. 14:13). Even though he was created perfectly and in beauty, this wickedness came from his very core. It was also premeditated and calculated as denoted from the phrase "multitude of thy merchandise" and the use of the word "reason" in the following passage (Ezek. 28:16-17):

> By the multitude of thy merchandise they have filled the midst of thee with violence, and thou hast sinned: therefore I will cast thee as profane out of the mountain of God: and I will destroy thee, O covering cherub, from the midst of the stones of fire. Thine heart was lifted up because of thy beauty, thou hast corrupted thy wisdom by reason of thy brightness: I will cast thee to the ground, I will lay thee before kings, that they may behold thee.

Pride Is About the "I"

How about today's Christians? Have they done the best job in differentiating themselves from unbelievers with respect to the ever-present, but yet frequent, undetectability of pride? Sadly, far too many people's lives have revolved around "I will" statements. " I will do well in school." "I will make the Little League team." "I will go out on a date with that specific person." "I will go to this college." "I will get this job." "I will marry this person." "I will buy this car and house." "I will have this many children." "I will go to this church." "I will only speak to the people I like." "I will not listen to other points of view." Touched upon often throughout this exploration will be the fundamental concept that pride is all about the "I" and the "me."

The Biblical account not only showcases that Satan is filled with pride but also lays the foundation for Satan's future mode of operation in the world. It sets in motion the abominable and heinous sin of pride that has been pervasive throughout the course of humanity.

> "It (pride) is one of Satan's chief modes of operation and favorite weapons of warfare *because it tempts us to take our eyes off God and place them on ourselves.*"[4] [My addition: LR]

Satan did not waste too much human time in implementing his snares and schemes.

Satan's Pride and Envy Displayed

Prior to the rebellion, this created spirit-being (still Lucifer) had also witnessed the creation of two other slightly "lesser" beings called humans (one man and one woman). These beings were created in the lovely image of their Maker and had been given dominion over every other living being that moved on the created Earth. They were given full provision for prosperous existence without having to work for it! They were even allowed to reproduce, which was not a privilege bestowed upon the so-called "greater" being, Lucifer. Creator God had specified only one simple restriction which was accompanied with a clear, dire warning for disobedience.

> *And the LORD God commanded the man, saying, Of every tree of the garden thou mayest freely eat: But of the tree of the knowledge of good and evil, thou shalt not eat of it: for in the day that thou eatest thereof thou shalt surely die. (Gen. 2:16-17)*

After the rebellion, the created being (now Satan), could no longer tolerate other beings receiving considerations that he did not receive. The very pride that led to his insurrection was now manifesting itself in blatant, full-blown envy. The comparative nature of his iniquitous self-importance reared its ugly head once more. Not only did his arrogance allow him to harbor enmity against God, but now, it was being unveiled against the two eternally-living

---

[4] Charles Stanley, <u>Landmines in the Path of the Believer</u> (Nashville, TN: Thomas Nelson, 2007), 15.

humans. He may have thought, "How can I simultaneously ruin these two beings, get back at the Creator and start my program for world dominance?" The idea came to him soon enough. He would execute a second trading and trafficking campaign to appeal to their pride. Why not? He had already been successful at waging a similar operation with one-third of his brethren. And as before, the approach had to be discreet or as the Holy Bible states, "subtle." As with his comrades, the victims could not be forced to rebel or it would not succeed on all fronts.

The Execution of Satan's Plan

The plan now needed execution. The first step would be to cleverly transform himself and take on the form of even a lesser created being; a serpent. Once disguised, the next phase was to cast doubt upon God's directives through a misrepresentation of His very Words. Satan easily accomplished this by eliminating the latter half of God's instructions and quoting a "half-truth." The Serpent asked,

> *"Yea, hath God said, Ye shall not eat of every tree of the garden?"*

(This Satanic approach is seen today in numerous Bible versions that add and remove the jots and tittles of God's Words.) When the initial distortion did not entirely work, his next and final step was to deliberately misrepresent. The Serpent voiced,

> *"Ye shall not surely die: For God doth know that in the day ye eat thereof, then your eyes shall be opened, and ye shall be as gods, knowing good and evil."(Gen. 3:4-5)*

His direct attack appealed to the "lust of the flesh, the lust of the eyes and the pride of life" (1 John 2:16). Not only did the fruit itself appear delicious and pleasant to the eyes but the tree itself was desirable for acquiring wisdom. The woman first succumbed in eating the fruit, soon to be followed by the man.

> *And when the woman saw that the tree was good for food, and that it was pleasant to the eyes, and a tree to be*

desired to make one wise, she took of the fruit thereof, and did eat, and gave also unto her husband with her; and he did eat. (Gen. 3:6)

The Fall of Man is Linked to Pride

Most people would accurately identify this account as the Biblical record of the "Fall of Man" in the Garden of Eden. Some refer to it as the account of "original sin." It is undeniably the description of what sin is and how it was imputed into humanity. It is not an allegory or a fable, as some who prefer to deny the Bible's inerrancy and inspiration, claim. The account clearly illustrates how Adam and Eve were given everything. Everything except one thing, or so they thought. It also shows how they desired to be all-seeing and all-knowing...to be as gods. This desire was nothing less than the sin of pride and of self-exaltation. It was when man and Satan first resembled each other.

"All of the evils of fallen angels and men have their birth in the pride of self."[5]

Results of the Fall

Their sin immediately drove humanity and earth into a state of death, curses, and suffering, all of which are still being experienced today. The Scriptures are clear that humankind will continue to experience a fallen world until the Abrahamic and Davidic Covenants are prophetically fulfilled by God through the establishment of Christ's literal Millennial Kingdom.

Secondarily, the "Fall of Man" is also a record of how the most self-centered being, Satan, was able to utilize his intimate knowledge of pride to infiltrate God's perfect creation. He soon realized that pride causes man to emphasize himself more than God, as the passage firmly establishes Satan's primary use of subtle temptation tactics leading to the sin of pride (Gen. 3:1-5). No doubt, he is relentless in this line of attack. Believers must never forget

---

[5] Andrew Murray, <u>Humility</u> (New Kensington, PA: Whitaker, 1982), 118.

that Satan (and his legions) is not yet literally or allegorically bound. He is still the "Prince of the Power of the Air" (Eph.2:2). The Bible testifies that Satan is still hindering (1 Thess. 2:18), buffeting (2 Cor. 12:7), working certain miracles (Rev. 16:14), filling hearts with lies (Acts 5:3), exhibiting power (Acts 26:18), blinding the minds of unbelievers (2 Cor. 4:4), taking away God's Words from the hearts of unbelievers (Luke 8:12; Mark 4:15), using world systems (1 John 2:15-17), tempting (1 Cor. 7:5; 1 Thess. 3:5), casting some into prison for witnessing (Rev. 2:10), destroying the flesh (1 Cor. 5:5), using devices for his advantage (2 Cor. 2:11), turning aside people after him (1 Tim 5:15), transforming himself into an angel of light (2 Cor. 11:14) and walking, seeking and devouring (1 Pet. 5:8) Therefore, the following warning is still binding. *"Be sober, be vigilant; because your adversary the devil, as a roaring lion, walketh about, seeking whom he may devour."* (1 Pet. 5:8)

CHAPTER 2

SETTING THE STAGE FOR PRIDE

Fast forwarding some 6,000 years or so, one can easily experience how the sin of pride is powerful and ubiquitous. As such, it will be useful to explore how it became rooted.

The Push to Excel

If you were a young man being raised in a 1970's working class, non-Christian home, you were probably raised with the all-important belief that excelling in many areas of life was of utmost significance. This is how you "got ahead" in life. Excellence associated with scholarship, athletics, supplementary activities, and all forms of social dealings, which included family, friendships, and of course, dating, was encouraged and emphasized. This focus on achievement ran through the fabric of most interactions. Sadly, the prime driver for this behavior came from parents who lived for the success of their children. Position and honor from other relatives and friends became paramount. Children's exploits became the parent's exploits. Rarely, if ever, were any taught that the sole reason for success was derived from the blessings bestowed by our Lord God. Therefore, it was not surprising that self-absorption (a.k.a. pride) was quickly and effectively transferred through osmosis since no one overtly taught anyone to be brash and abrasive.

Pride and the Loss of Humility

As expected, this lacking of God's presence, combined with worldly stimuli (along with the "flesh"), naturally bred an absence of humility. That absence of humility quickly spread to many, if not all, forms of interaction. It infiltrated conversation, behaviors, and thoughts. The masses were unaware that it would certainly become the gateway for many other issues.

> "And so pride, or the loss of humility, is the root of every sin and evil."[6]

> "Pride is the root for many of our sinful thoughts and actions."[7]

A Significant Area of Pride: Athletics

One area of pride's clear manifestation was in the participation of athletic events. Pride led competitors to an overwhelming desire to win. This overpowering desire for victory subsequently led to a heightened level of intensity. This intensity in competition soon created an environment where losing gracefully, or even winning gracefully, became rarer and rarer as the competition's importance grew in meaning and stature. It has been said that:

> "Pride based on the world's values always breeds competition, which leads to division and strife."[8]

The Consequences of Improper Attitude

This sort of division and strife is an all too frequent occurrence in sporting events. However, this "sore loser" or "sore winner" attitude was not especially frowned upon as long as it was kept within the bounds of that era's acceptable civility. Driving this attitude was the belief that winners get something that losers do not get. This something does not have to be anything tangible like a trophy or cash winnings, it may just be the inner satisfaction that you were victorious and your opponent was not.

The Performance of the Individual Exalted

Even winning as a team began to take second place to individual performance. Statistical tallying of goals, points, assists, touchdowns, homeruns, field goals, rebounds and singles became more interesting than wins and losses. The ability to quickly recite these individual achievements

---

[6] Andrew Murray, <u>Humility</u> (New Kensington, PA: Whitaker, 1982), 16.
[7] Charles Stanley, <u>Landmines in the Path of the Believer</u> (Nashville, TN: Thomas Nelson, 2007), 25.
[8] Ibid., 27.

was all too common and became a means to remind others of how invaluable you really were. From these relatively small and insignificant experiences as young men, it is not hard to understand how today's athletes became engrossed with bringing attention to self.

A full generation later, one only need watch a few minutes of a professional sporting event to witness the thriving of pride's malevolence and deceptiveness. This thriving is seen through self-centered celebrations, poor sportsmanship, hyper-fanaticism, sexualized cheer-leaders, ideological sponsorships, and alcohol consumption. A well-known former coach and Christian writes,

> "As a society, we claim that we like the quiet, humble athlete, but in reality, those aren't the guys that get the focus – at least not as much as the guys who are trying to bring attention to their own names."[9]

Christians Guilty of Subsidizing Worldly Events

Looking in the mirror, Christians are also to blame for befriending (financially and time-wise) worldly events that endeavor to sanitize self-aggrandizement. The Body of Christ must pray that Christians hopefully think twice (or better pray) before embracing certain events.

Another Significant Area Producing Pride: Academics

Similar to athletics, academics became a source of pride. Receiving good grades or winning a spelling bee became synonymous with receiving accolades from parents, extended family, and friends. Pride was also evident in the reciting of learned data. Interestingly, pride even permeated low points in scholastic endeavor. Average grades were simply dismissed as a result of not really wanting to do well. The patent response was: "I can do well anytime I set my mind to it." Therefore, *pride's insidiousness showed itself in*

---

[9] Tony Dungy, <u>Uncommon</u> (Carol Stream, IL: Tyndale House, 2009), 18.

mediocrity or even failure! Doing poorly was rationalized and simply became another vehicle to bring attention to self.

Of course, athletics and academics were not the only channels promoted by Satan to bring glory to oneself; they just happen to be two of the more prominent ones. Physical appearance, family status, profession, material possessions (including home), types of vacations, and schools attended are just a few of the common platforms for self-promotion.

Some Useful Qualities in Athletics and Academics

For the sake of clarity, sometimes athletics, and especially academics, have some redeeming and useful qualities. Knowledge acquired through formal education has been mightily used by God over the centuries. The Jewish Scribes and Priests were educated men that maintained, copied, read and taught the Words of God. Moses was a learned man of Egypt who was able to lead the Israelites for forty years and pen the Pentateuch. Paul of Tarsus was a former Pharisee who was able to teach infallible doctrine while laying the framework for Christian apologetics still being used today. Luke was a physician who travelled with Paul and meticulously wrote the Gospel of Luke and the Acts of the Apostles. Matthew was a tax collector who eventually wrote a synoptic Gospel that bears his name. Even with regards to athletics, several (like Eric Liddell) were able to provide millions of unsaved people with a godly, Christian testimony. Even the same Paul conveyed that exercise has some merit (1 Tim. 4:8).

The Thesis of This Work

The stated position is, however, that self-exaltation and boasting can firmly establish itself in the hearts and minds of children by the use of these two very prominent worldly venues. The following three verses directly address the self-adulation that comes from physical strength and knowledge.

Lo, this is the man that made not God his strength; but trusted in the abundance of his riches, and strengthened himself in his wickedness. (Ps. 52:7)

Knowledge puffeth up. (1 Cor. 8:1)

Woe unto them that are wise in their own eyes, and prudent in their own sight! (Isa. 5:21)

Hence, one can be steadfast in the assessment that knowledge and physical ability, while not the only ones, are two of the most used triggers to procure and feed feelings of superiority.

A Remnant of Humility

Even in that climate of hubris [which is pride that leads to arrogance], there still existed a remnant of humility in society. It was mostly expected that parents, relatives, teachers, and law enforcement were to be respected. Hence, a form of submission to authority still existed. The obvious error was that no reason was given as to why authority had to be respected other than the fact that it was the correct thing to do. Failure to comply was often met with some form of reprisal. Unfortunately, these punishments were inconsistently applied and, most importantly, not tied to the original source of Holy Scripture. It is disappointing to note that the humble remnant in society continues to discernibly shrink since that time. This should not surprise Bible-believing and Bible-reading Christians.

Pride Linked to the Last Days

God's Words are unwavering in declaring that the increase in self-love, boasting, and pride, are undeniably linked with the" last" days:

This know also, that in the last days perilous times shall come. For men shall be lovers of their own selves, covetous, boasters, proud, blasphemers, disobedient to parents, unthankful, unholy, Without natural affection, trucebreakers, false accusers, incontinent, fierce, despisers of those that are good, Traitors, heady, highminded, lovers of pleasures more than lovers of

God; Having a form of godliness, but denying the power thereof: from such turn away. (2 Tim. 3:1-5)

While the account just conveyed reflects a non-Christian experience, it can also be applied to some of the experiences in the Christian community of yesterday.

Some Christians Strive For Invalid "Virtues"

Sadly, some Christians (or ones that simply called themselves such) only strove for the virtues that were commonly celebrated in the secular world. Virtues such as boldness (just-do-it), joy (be happy), and zeal (support the local sports team) were given pre-eminence. These virtues, without the cloaking of humility, eventually transformed themselves into just another platform where the proud could show-off to others, extolling their beliefs and abilities.

So the stage was set. The seeds of haughtiness were sown in hearts. These very hearts were bound to thoughts of desire and worldly ambition. Self-exaltation not only showed itself in the highs and successes of life, but also revealed itself in the low points and struggles of life. It showed itself in homes of believers and unbelievers alike. *It likewise showed itself in the mundane aspects of life as the daily routine became mainly a ritual of self.* Unknown to most was that a life-pattern was being established that would later be filled with all of the subtle (and sometimes not so subtle) manifestations of pride.

Many were sadly either unaware that modesty and arrogance could not coexist, or chose to ignore the warnings of letting the latter take over one's life. These haughty and prideful manifestations were soon to be followed by painful consequences of which God had long ago admonished the world.

Definitions of Pride and Humility Corrupted

One of the results was that the definitions of pride and humility became corrupted. Most had no idea what they meant. Ask the average person today and you will experience a potpourri of answers, very few of which are biblically based. Is it a virtue or vice or neither? Not surprisingly, your worldview will affect how these questions are answered. These questions and their corresponding worldviews shall be explored in the next chapter.

CHAPTER 3

VIRTUE, VICE: MEAN OR NICE?

The Biblical and World Definitions Differ

A conventional first step in examining the themes of pride and humility is to compare how the world and the Bible define them. However, even before the terms are defined there should be agreement that one is clearly a virtue (humility) and the other is clearly a sin against God and man (pride). As we shall see, the Holy Bible is firm and unanimous in its categorization of both.

The Biblical Definition

Regarding pride, the Bible inextricably connects it to wickedness (Psa. 10:2-4) and evil (Prov. 8:13). In fact, God's Words call a "high look" and a "proud heart," sin (Prov. 21:4). It is not surprising then that God hates pride (Prov. 8:13) and declares explicitly that one should not be proud (Jer. 13:15).

Pride Is Not From God, But Man

First John 2:16 makes certain that pride does not come from God:

> *For all that is in the world, the lust of the flesh, and the lust of the eyes, and the pride of life, is not of the Father, but is of the world.*

But if not from God, then where does pride come from? Mark 7:21-23 shows how pride (and other sins that God hates) comes from within man's heart. The book of Proverbs also reveals what God feels about pride:

> *Every one that is proud in heart is an abomination to the LORD: though hand join in hand, he shall not be unpunished. (Prov. 16:5)*

In this respect, man is similar to Satan since pride emanates from the heart of both.

Romans 1:29-31 provides a very comprehensive list of sins to which pride and boasting are clearly associated. Through the Holy Spirit's inspiration, the Apostle Paul writes:

> *Being filled with all unrighteousness, fornication, wickedness, covetousness, maliciousness; full of envy, murder, debate, deceit, malignity; whisperers, Backbiters, haters of God, despiteful, proud, boasters, inventors of evil things, disobedient to parents, Without understanding, covenant breakers, without natural affection, implacable, unmerciful.*

God Hates Pride

Through these non-exhaustive set of verses, one can confidently and unmistakably state that the Lord hates pride, and thusly pride can be categorized as a sin and a vice. Even within this "infamous" list of sins, pride and boastfulness distinguish themselves. A quote from "Humility: The Forgotten Virtue" best illustrates the point.

> "Most sins turn us away from God, but pride is a direct attack upon God. It lifts our hearts above Him. Pride seeks to dethrone God and enthrone self."[10]

Humility Is a Command From God

Humility, on the other hand, is a virtue that is commanded from God. He calls saints to be humble.

> *Humble yourselves therefore under the mighty hand of God, that he may exalt you in due time. (1 Pet. 5:6)*

The Behavior & Blessings Associated With Humility

In addition, there are many verses that illustrate the behaviors and corresponding Godly blessings for those that possess a humble heart and obey God. The humble will seek God's face (2 Chron. 7:14), will seek the Lord in all matters (Zeph. 2:3), and in all times of affliction (2 Chron. 33:12). The truly humble will therefore seek God in prayer throughout the day. This seeking is done in times of

---

[10] Wayne Mack, <u>Humility: The Forgotten Virtue</u> (Phillipsburg, NJ: P&R Publishing, 2005), 9.

abundance and joy or in times of scarcity and weeping. They will also seek to read His pure Words as often as possible. This should translate into having an insatiable desire to spend more time with Him! In the end, he or she knows that it is not possible to live this temporal existence without God's assistance. Moreover, it is impossible to Biblically dispute that God does not favor a humble spirit when His Words show that God will guide and teach (Psa. 25:9), give grace (Jas 4:6), remember (Psa. 9:12; 136:23) and will exalt those that are humble (Matt. 23:12; Luke 1:52; 14:11; 18:14; 1 Pet. 5:6; Jas. 1:9). Based on this short list of many more applicable verses, one can without hesitation (but not proudly!), state that humility is a virtue.

Unfortunately, even with clear and overwhelming Scriptural and empirical evidence, the deluded will still call good evil and evil good (Isa. 5:20). By the Holy Spirit, Solomon writes,

> *"Fools make a mock at sin: but among the righteous there is favour." (Prov. 14:9)*

Therefore it is not surprising that the secular world views pride and humility very differently than the Bible views them.

The Self-Esteem Industry

Without much investigation one can easily discern that pride has been embraced by the world system as the good and right thing to have. Most people view pride as a necessary ingredient for worldly success. They ask, "How can a person have a successful career, meet an attractive spouse, or deal with life's challenges without pride?" Even further, led by secular social scientists, many have deceptively attributed the ills of today's society to a lack of pride or self-esteem among its members. In essence, it has become the root for almost every form of interpersonal issue. To combat this societal ill of low self-esteem/pride, a major industry solely focused on promoting aspects of self (esteem, improvement, and glory) has become a profitable world fixture. Books, CDs, DVDs, seminars and retreats that focus on a variety of wellness programs can be found everywhere. It can almost go without saying that this industry is selling a solution that focuses on how one can independently become a complete individual. (The twisted irony is that one cannot be independent of the self-esteem guru!) In general, the world has lost touch with the idea that pride and self-love are very destructive and manifestation of these is when humans are most like the Devil, as concluded earlier. Not only does pride strive to eliminate God's presence and power from lives, but it also subtly places mankind at enmity with God by embracing the worship of self. A familiar quote illustrates this belief:

"I am no more humble than my talents require."[11]

If Jesus Christ had felt this way he would not have had an ounce of humility.

Selfism and Pride

Selfism is not the only form of pride celebrated by the secular world. In the last forty years, the word, pride, has been used by racial and ethnic groups (Black pride, Hispanic pride, Asian pride, Irish pride, etc.) to try to instill a false sense of increased self-worth. They do not mention that true self-worth has already been given to all by God as He created man in His own image (Gen. 1:26, 27; 9:6; Rom. 8:29; Col. 3:10). The *whole world* is also *given* the opportunity to be sons and daughters of God through the free saving grace of Lord Jesus Christ by repenting, believing and living for Him (John 1:12; Rom. 8:14; 1 John 3:1-2). *The only way to achieve long lasting self-worth and peace is to know that you will be with God the Father and Jesus Christ throughout eternity*!

---

[11] Oscar Levant. www.finestquotes.com. http://www.finestquotes.com/author_quotes-author-Oscar%20Levant page-0.htm (accessed January 8, 2011).

Pride and Perverse Groups

The word pride has also been hijacked by several sexually perverse groups. It is now difficult to find a corporation or government agency that has not engaged in some sort of "Gay Pride" celebration. In a bizarre way, militant homosexual groups have actually correctly used pride when cloning phrases like Gay and Lesbian pride. These groups have combined two sins which are both described by God as vile abominations.

> *Who changed the truth of God into a lie, and worshipped and served the creature more than the Creator, who is blessed for ever. Amen. For this cause God gave them up unto vile affections: for even their women did change the natural use into that which is against nature: And likewise also the men, leaving the natural use of the woman, burned in their lust one toward another; men with men working that which is unseemly, and receiving in themselves that recompence of their error which was meet. (Rom. 1:25-27)*

As will be soon demonstrated, a proud person will be led into other types of sin. In some cases, the unrepentant sinner will even try to justify and rationalize their sin using false science ("we were born that way"), pleas of compassion ("we just want to be loved and get married like anyone else"), and so-called psychological intimidation ("you are an intolerant hater").

Self and Evangelical Christianity

Tragically, the worship of self has also found its way into Evangelical Christianity. Painfully, this "Christian" experience has become more prevalent as the church now emulates the unsaved world in ways which would have been unheard of a generation ago. The Emergent Church, The New Apostolic Reformation, liberal "Mainline" denominations, Hyper-Pentecostalism, Liberation Theology and Neo-Evangelicalism are a few of the guilty suspects. The following quotes best sum it up:

> "From countless sources, claims are heard that

> God's great design for His people is health, prosperity, success, happiness, and self-fulfillment." "The Bible's teaching of suffering and cross-bearing for Christ's sake are either ignored altogether or foolishly explained away." "A weak gospel, easy believism, and nonsacrificial Christian living are the reflections of this new "evangelical" selfism...It has (church teaching) replaced sacrifice with success, suffering with self-satisfaction, and godly obedience with fleshly indulgence."[12]

On a similar note, the secular world has also defined humility and its siblings, meekness and gentleness, as signs of weakness. Very few want to turn the other cheek as Christ commanded (Matt. 5:39; Luke 6:29) or be viewed as a doormat that constantly forgives others (as in 490 times in Matt. 18:22). In contrast, the character traits of aggressiveness, quick wittedness, strength, articulateness and boldness are all viewed by many secularists (and some Christians) as much more important than humility. "Humility is no substitute for a good personality"[13] is a quote that only few might accept consciously but many more accept subconsciously. This is played out frequently in elections as many people will vote for style over substance. (The 2008 Presidential election comes to mind!) For many, it even comes into play when selecting a spouse.

Some find it so difficult to become humble that they give up on the possibility of ever attaining it. Famous architect Frank Lloyd Wright said, "Early in life I had to choose between honest arrogance and hypocritical humility. I chose the former and have seen no reason to change."[14] It was too bad that Mr. Wright limited his choices between two evils. He either never read the Bible or read it but did not

---

[12] John MacArthur, The MacArthur New Testament Commentary (Nashville, TN: Thomas Nelson, 2007), Matthew 20:20-28.

[13] Fran Lebowitz. www.finestquotes.com. http://www.finestquotes.com/author_quotes-author Fran%20Lebowitz-page-1.htm (accessed January 8, 2011).

[14] Ibid., Frank Lloyd Wright. http://www.finestquotes.com/author_quotes-author-Frank%20Lloyd%20Wright page-1.htm (accessed January 8, 2011).

believe its consequences and rewards/blessings. Another quote that depicts the world's view of humility is:

> "The proud man can learn humility, but he will be proud of it"[15]

Even Ben Franklin said,

> "Pride is said to be the last vice the good man gets clear of."[16]

While attaining true humility is trying, Scripture is clear that it can be attained. If it were not so, God would be made a liar. The Lord Jesus would not have asked believers to do things that could not have been possible!

> *. . . Verily I say unto you, Except ye be converted, and become as little children, ye shall not enter into the kingdom of heaven. Whosoever therefore shall humble himself as this little child, the same is greatest in the kingdom of heaven. (Matt. 18:3-4)*

---

[15] Mignon McLaughlin. www.brainyquote.com. http://www.brainyquote.com/quotes/keywords/humility_5.html (accessed January 8, 2011).

[16] Benjamin Franklin. www.finestquotes.com. http://www.finestquotes.com/quote_with-keyword-Pride-page 5.htm (accessed January 8, 2011).

CHAPTER 4

PROPERLY & BIBLICALLY DEFINED

As confirmed from several prior examples, the world now calls pride good and calls humility evil. Even Christians are not exempt. Not surprisingly, Satan continues to twist God's Words until they are unrecognizable from the original meaning. For that reason, it would be beneficial to now examine how the Bible defines both terms.

As noted earlier, pride is viewed by God as a sin and an abomination. There are many other words and phrases found in Scripture that also describe a proud spirit that are unmistakably unflattering. They are: arrogance, swelling, highness, haughtiness, puffed-up, vainglory, conceit, an attitude of a lion, wolves, boaster, boast against, pompous, to inflate with self-conceit, to rise, to soar, to be lofty, to be higher, make high, highminded, to lift up, mount up, upward, loud, presumptuous, appearing above others, glorying, rejoice against, to vaunt and exalt. *At its foundation, pride is the unwillingness to consider oneself nothing, to be considered nothing, and to submit absolutely to God.*

The Anthropocentric Definitions

Outside of Scripture, many faithful and accurate definitions of pride exist. What follows are a few of them.

> "Prideful people believe that all things should be from them, through them, and to them or for them."[17]

> "Pride glorifies man and robs God of the glory that only he deserves."[18]

> "The mindset of self (a master's mindset rather

---

[17] Stuart Scott, <u>From Pride to Humility: A Biblical Perspective</u> (Bemidji, MN: Focus Publishing Incorporated, 2010), 5.

[18] Warren Wiersbe, <u>The Strategy of Satan</u> (Carol Stream, IL: Tyndale House Publishers, 1979), 55.

than that of a servant): a focus on self and the service of self, a pursuit of self-recognition and self-exaltation, and a desire to control and use all things for self."[19]

"Pride is the elevation of self at the expense of God and His glory. It results in a self-serving lifestyle. Pride has no place for God. It takes credit for what God has done and given."[20]

"Pride is all about me."[21]

What do all of these definitions have in common? They would all be unambiguously considered "Anthropocentric," which is the belief that all things revolve around man. This belief represents the essential philosophies of humanism, atheism and evolutionism. It is Satanic to its very core!

The Sting of Pride

Predictably, most people have a very difficult time admitting and confessing that they have pride in their heart. This admission may only come after an explanation of what pride truly is in hearts and lives. Even believers typically recoil at the idea that they have no place for God, or that they are elevating themselves above an Omnipotent and Holy God. They would be more apt to admit to lying, gossiping, stealing, blaspheming, being unforgiving, etc., than pride. *The irony is how the sin of pride seems to sting the ego of Christians. A possible reason for this may come from the fact that pride is often forgotten or neglected since it is always operating at a foundational level.* It practically becomes part of the "woodwork" of daily existence. It must be remembered that Satan's most damaging work is done under the cloak of craftiness and stealth.

"If Satan can get you to act and think independently of God's will, he can then control your will and control your life. You will think you are acting freely,

---

[19] Stuart Scott, <u>From Pride to Humility: A Biblical Perspective</u> (Bemidji, MN: Focus Publishing Incorporated, 2010), 6.

[20] Joseph Stowell, <u>Tongue in Check</u> (Wheaton, IL: Victor Books, 1983), 77.

[21] Tony Dungy, <u>Uncommon</u> (Carol Stream, IL: Tyndale House, 2009), 19.

which is part of Satan's deception; but actually you will be acting under orders from the ruler of this world."[22]

This quote is not speaking of demon possession since that cannot happen to a Holy Spirit filled saint. It basically speaks of Satan introducing circumstances into lives whereby man simply acts on them in a carnal and fleshly manner. It is alarming to note how many born-again believers are still operating at this level.

Three Ways To Live Life

All must remember that there are three ways man can live his life. Man can choose to live for himself alone and satisfy the lusts of the flesh; he can be influenced by the world system, of which Satan is the Prince, or he can be surrendered to God. Man has free will to choose but God's way is the more excellent way. Lest one overlooks that God's ways are perfect, the Bible states:

> *He is the Rock, his work is perfect: for all his ways are judgment: a God of truth and without iniquity, just and right is he. (Deut. 32:4)*

The Need for Prayer

Beloved Christian, earnestly pray to God to search your heart of this evil and make you aware of its presence. Subsequently pray to God for guidance in ridding you of the odiousness of pride.

Common Definitions of Pride

Returning to definitions, *Webster's 1913 Dictionary* offers an extensive definition of pride in its noun form. It reads:

> The quality or state of being proud; inordinate self-esteem; an unreasonable conceit of one's own superiority in talents, beauty, wealth, rank, etc., which manifests itself in lofty airs, distance, reserve, and often in contempt of others. A sense of one's own worth, and

---

[22] Warren Wiersbe, <u>The Strategy of Satan</u> (Carol Stream, IL: Tyndale House Publishers, 1979), 57.

> abhorrence of what is beneath or unworthy of one; lofty self-respect; noble self-esteem; elevation of character; dignified bearing; proud delight; - in a good sense. Proud or disdainful behavior or treatment; insolence or arrogance of demeanor; haughty bearing and conduct; insolent exultation; disdain. That of which one is proud; that which excites boasting or self-gratulation; the occasion or ground of self-esteem, or of arrogant and presumptuous confidence, as beauty, ornament, noble character, children, etc. Show; ostentation; glory.[23]

From this all-encompassing definition one should admit, "The question is not, 'Do I have it?' but, 'Where is it?' and 'How much of it do I have?'"

More recent definitions have been corrupted by the world since it is the author's belief that dictionaries are also an area of demonic attack. An example of this corruption is found in a portion of *The Free Dictionary*'s modern definition of pride. It offers a very different and more convoluted meaning than the one presented in Webster's 1913 version. It reads:

> A sense of one's own proper dignity or value; self-respect; Pleasure or satisfaction taken in an achievement, possession, or association: parental pride; Arrogant or disdainful conduct or treatment; haughtiness; A cause or source of pleasure or satisfaction; the best of a group or class: These soldiers were their country's pride; The most successful or thriving condition; prime: the pride of youth.[24]

The Exact Opposite Virtue: Humility

As noted earlier, humility or being humble is considered a virtue by God and as such will be the exact opposite or antonym of pride. There are many Biblical words and phrases that are often used synonymously to define humility. They are: Meek(ness), low, low degree/estate, lowliness, abase, crouch, poor, subdue, submit, modest(y),

---

[23] www.webster-dictionary.org. http://www.webster-dictionary.org/definition/pride (accessed January 8, 2011).

[24] http://www.thefreedictionary.com/Pride (accessed January 6, 2011).

casted down, self-affliction, incline, bow, kneel, mild(ness), gentle(ness), depressed, dove, lamb and sheep. *Foundationally, humility is the ongoing acceptance to consider oneself nothing, to be considered nothing by others and to submit all absolutely to a Holy, Righteous God.*

As with pride, several accurate definitions of humility exist outside of Scripture.

> "Humility is to make a right estimate of one's self. It is no humility for a man to think less of himself than he ought, though it might rather puzzle him to do that."[25]

> "Humility is the call to all earnest Christians to prove that meekness and lowliness of heart are the chief marks by which they follow the meek and humble Lamb of God."[26]

> "Humility, the place of entire dependence on God."[27]

> "Humility means giving up of self and becoming perfect nothingness before God."[28]

> "The mindset of Christ (a servant's mindset): a focus on God and others, a pursuit of the recognition and the exaltation of God, and a desire to glorify and please God in all things and by all things He has given."[29]

Webster's 1913 dictionary defines humility as:

> "The state or quality of being humble; freedom from pride and arrogance; lowliness of mind; a modest estimate of one's own worth; a sense of one's own unworthiness through imperfection and sinfulness; self-

---

[25] Charles Haddon Spurgeon. www.finestquotes.com. http://www.finestquotes.com/author_quotes-author Charles%20H.%20Spurgeon-page-0.htm (accessed January 8, 2011).

[26] Andrew Murray, Humility (New Kensington, PA: Whitaker, 1982), 119.

[27] Ibid., 16.

[28] Ibid., 92.

[29] Stuart Scott, From Pride to Humility: A Biblical Perspective (Bemidji, MN: Focus Publishing Incorporated, 2010), 18.

abasement; humbleness. An act of submission or courtesy."[30]

Conversely, all of these definitions would be considered "Theocentric" because they are God centered. All is from, by and through God.

The Definitive Biblical Definition of Humility

From the author's point-of-view, a definitive Biblical meaning of humility can be found in the fifth chapter of Paul's second letter to the Corinthians. Paul writes:

> *For the love of Christ constraineth us; because we thus judge, that if one died for all, then were all dead: And that he died for all, that they which live should not henceforth live unto themselves, but unto him which died for them, and rose again. (2 Cor. 5:14-15)*

This lovely passage declares that man should no longer live for himself but for the risen Lord and Savior Jesus Christ! *Living for Him becomes the genuine basis for humility.* It embodies the true and mature believer's way of living. Christ's humility and teachings, as well as Biblical solutions to pride's persistent presence, will be covered later in the exploration.

Meanings Found in the Original Languages

Before moving further, it would be prudent to look at the original canonical languages to gain further insight into the definitions of pride and humility. Interestingly, some fascinating truths are uncovered upon close inspection.

Hebrew

Pride

First, reviewing the underlying Hebrew Masoretic texts, it is disclosed that pride and its synonyms are found in over sixty words. The first etymological connection is made

---

[30] www.webster-dictionary.org. http://www.webster-dic tionary.org/definition/humility (accessed January 8, 2011).

with the root adjective "גא" (transliteration: gē[31]). Meaning proud or haughty, it is found twenty-two times in various forms throughout the King James Version. One of its uses is found in the book of Isaiah. The prophet pens:

> *We have heard of the pride of Moab; he is very proud:*
> *even of his haughtiness, and his pride, and his wrath:*
> *but his lies shall not be so. (Isa. 16:6)*

It is interesting to note that the word to denote evil pride in Hebrew is phonetically pronounced in English as gā. Who knew that when you pronounce "gay" in Hebrew it can mean haughtiness or homosexual (if the English trans-literation is used)! As stated earlier, it is nothing short of combining two sins which God hates.

Another interesting relationship is found with the Hebrew root verb "רהב"[32] which is transliterated rāhab (pronounced: raw-hab'). Most often defined as proud or behaving proudly, one of the derivatives of this Hebrew word is utilized to describe the country of Egypt because of their arrogance and opulence over the centuries.

The last intriguing Hebrew note with regard to pride, is found with the adjective "רנמה"[33]. Transliterated as rômâ and meaning haughtily, this Hebrew word is pronounced exactly the same as Rome is pronounced in Latin. It is difficult to ignore the phonetic association between a word that means haughtily and a city that behaved pompously and eventually fell due to those very excesses.

With respect to humility and its varied synonyms, there are over twenty Hebrew words used throughout the Old Testament. One of the more frequently used words is "כנע"[34]. A primitive root which is transliterated kāna (pronounced: kaw-nah'), it is translated thirty-six times in

---

[31] James Strong, *Strong's Talking Greek & Hebrew Dictionary*, (Austin, TX: WORD*search* Corp., 2007), WORD*search* CROSS e-book, Under: "H1341"

[32] Ibid., Under: "H7292".

[33] Ibid., Under: "H7317".

[34] Ibid., Under: "H3665".

the King James Version mostly as humble or to subdue. The original meaning is to humiliate, vanquish or to bend the knee.

Greek

Pride

Looking now at the underlying Greek Received Texts or "Textus Receptus," one finds a couple of curious associations. Considering pride and its synonyms, two expressions seem to "stand-out" above the others. The first word "καυχάομαι"[35] offers the most frequent usage of boasting and glorying to be found in the New Testament. Transliterated kauchaomai (pronounced: kow-khah'-om-ahee) it is used thirty-eight times in both good and evil connotations. The most well-known use of this term is located in Ephesians 2:9: "Not of works, lest any man should boast." The second word, while only used once in the New Testament (2 Tim. 3:2), deserves mention due to its uniqueness. The Greek Word "φίλαυτος" (transliterated: philautos)[36] means love of self. Many people can readily identify the "phil" with the city of Philadelphia (called the city of brotherly love) and "autos" which is a carriage (automobile) that moves itself.

Humility

The only Greek synonym for humility that will be mentioned is the verb "ὑποτάσσω" (transliterated: hypotassō and pronounced: hoop-ot-as'-so).[37] The term is used forty times in the New Testament to describe various forms of subjection and submission. Well-known uses of this word are found in James 4:7 ("Submit yourselves therefore to God. Resist the devil, and he will flee from you.") and in the Godly wife submission passages found in Ephesians 5:21-22 and 1 Peter 3:1-5.

---

[35] Ibid., Under: "G2744".
[36] Ibid., Under: "G5367".
[37] Ibid., Under: "G5293".

Now that pride and humility have been properly defined, a deeper exploration to determine if there is such a thing as "good" boasting would be valuable. And if there is such a thing as "good" boasting, what does the Bible have to say about it?

CHAPTER 5

GOOD BOASTING?

Taking a slight digression, one has to be careful not to force certain words into one classification even though the vast majority falls within that usage. A primary example of this comes with the words: boasting and glorying. As recognized earlier, Scripture generally uses these words to describe the sin of pride in Satan and man. However, there are several instances when good and Godly usage of these words is clearly indicated.

When Boasting Is Allowed

The most important area where boasting is good and allowable is when one is boasting and glorying in an Omnipotent and Righteous Father God. This can be the case even under adverse circumstances. King David offers one such example in Psalm 34:

> My soul shall make her boast in the LORD: the humble
> shall hear thereof, and be glad. O magnify the LORD
> with me, and let us exalt his name together. (Ps 34: 2-3)

Another such example is provided by the Apostle Paul as he wrote to the Corinthians:

> But we will not boast of things without our measure, but
> according to the measure of the rule which God hath
> distributed to us, a measure to reach even unto you. (2
> Cor. 10:13)

Several verses also condone boasting in our Lord and Saviour.

> That, according as it is written, He that glorieth, let him
> glory in the Lord. (1 Cor. 1:31)

> For though I should boast somewhat more of our
> authority, which the Lord hath given us for edification,
> and not for your destruction, I should not be ashamed. (2
> Cor. 10:8)

> *But he that glorieth, let him glory in the Lord. (2 Cor. 10:17)*

The Holy Bible also makes provision for saints to boast in the salvation and subsequent works of brothers and sisters in Christ. The prophet Isaiah provides one such illustration that is set in the Millennial Reign of Christ:

> *But ye shall be named the Priests of the LORD: men shall call you the Ministers of our God: ye shall eat the riches of the Gentiles, and in their glory shall ye boast yourselves. (Isa. 61:6)*

Likewise, Paul again provides several verses outlining the goodness of boasting in the body of living saints:

> *For we commend not ourselves again unto you, but give you occasion to glory on our behalf, that ye may have somewhat to answer them which glory in appearance, and not in heart. (2 Cor. 5:12)*

> *For if I have boasted any thing to him of you, I am not ashamed; but as we spake all things to you in truth, even so our boasting, which I made before Titus, is found a truth. (2 Cor. 7:14)*

> *For I know the forwardness of your mind, for which I boast of you to them of Macedonia, that Achaia was ready a year ago; and your zeal hath provoked very many. (2 Cor. 9:2)*

Lastly, *God makes provision for brethren to glory and boast during the most difficult times:*

> *And not only so, but we glory in tribulations also: knowing that tribulation worketh patience. (Rom. 5:3)*

> *And he said unto me, My grace is sufficient for thee: for my strength is made perfect in weakness. Most gladly therefore will I rather glory in my infirmities, that the power of Christ may rest upon me. (2 Cor. 12:9)*

Now that pride's meaning and its predominantly destructive usage have been carefully considered, it would be appropriate to delve deeper to faithfully consider its wide-ranging displays and manifestations.

CHAPTER 6

DISPLAYS AND MANIFESTATIONS OF PRIDE

Discernment and Pride

Obvious manifestations of pride can be seen and observed by most people. As the manifestation becomes more concealed, a more discerning eye or ear will be needed to identify the act. This discernment can only be attained as Christians go through the process of sanctification and be continually filled with the Holy Spirit. (The expectation being that mature believers will more readily identify pride in themselves and others.) The good news is that they may no longer exhibit blatant manifestations of pride. The bad news is that pride then goes "underground" often contorting itself into refined and understated expressions. So subtle are these expressions, that the possessor is frequently not aware of its residence in his or her heart. As such, the most subtle or secret ones will be known only by God as only He can search a man's heart:

> *Shall not God search this out? for he knoweth the secrets of the heart. (Psa. 44:21)*

> *And he that searcheth the hearts knoweth what is the mind of the Spirit, because he maketh intercession for the saints according to the will of God. (Rom. 8:27)*

Other Scriptures elucidating this truth are found in 1 Chron. 28:9 and Rev. 2:23. It should be noted that while the sin of pride is found in all people, no one will possess every manifestation of it. As shall be seen later, even men who walked with God had pride issues. Paradoxically, some of pride's manifestations are also its consequences further proving its insidiousness because of its circularity (a possible never ending loop).

Pride in the Heart and Open Rebellion

When man has pride in his heart, it always negatively impacts his relationship with the Holy God. The Bible teaches that prideful man, especially in his unregenerate state, will not seek God (Psa. 10:4; Hos. 7:10) and God is not in his thoughts (Psa. 10:4). Since he will not seek God, then it stands to reason that he will not hearken to His commandments (Neh. 9:16) and will undoubtedly err from them (Psa. 119:21). For the prideful, the Ten Commandments have become representative symbols that were part of an intolerant societal time. The "enlightened" are no longer held to task by these "outdated" codes of morality. God's Words thus call these misguided people *unholy* and *blasphemous* (2 Tim. 3:2) as many will worship idols and false gods (Psa. 97:7). Most often they are openly disobedient to God (Jer. 44:10) and think that they can do anything without Him (Isa. 9:9-12). This open rebellion and disdain for God allows them to be openly hedonistic (Isa 3:16) and lovers of pleasures much more than they would ever love the Holy Father (2 Tim. 3:4). In today's world, one can readily observe how people will try to sooth their guilty conscience by deluding themselves into believing that God does not exist or by philosophizing that His judgments are not righteous. God frequently becomes only a "bell-hop" to be called upon when something is needed or when there is a major crisis. A powerful quote illustrates this veracity:

> Pride strikes a friendship with God only when it is convenient; it established friendships that promote itself; it takes orders only from within, and it seeks the accumulation of wealth, status, fame and glory. Pride seeks to control at any cost and to accomplish its own end regardless of the price.[38]

It will only get worse according to God's Words:

> *Now the Spirit speaketh expressly, that in the latter times some shall depart from the faith, giving heed to seducing spirits, and doctrines of devils; Speaking lies in*

---

[38] Joseph Stowell , <u>Tongue in Check</u> (Wheaton, IL: Victor Books, 1983), 83.

hypocrisy; having their conscience seared with a hot iron. (1 Tim. 4:1-2)

A Form of Godliness

Mature Christians please take note. *While pride is a sin that all believers possess, it is also a mark of someone who has not been "born-again."* The Bible explicitly warns us that these unsaved and proud individuals will not be sitting home idly, but many will actually be "front and center" in churches. These "false brethren" could be faithful attendees and even be participating in ministries. Some may possess a form of godliness but will deny its true power (2 Tim. 3:5). Since in reality they are not close to God, this haughty group will think that worldly gain is godliness (1 Tim. 6:5). They will even magnify themselves against God's people (Zeph. 2:9-11) and at some point will despise those that are good (2 Tim. 3:3). Initially concealed, their contempt against those that are good will be unmistakable when opposed. Rick Warren's "The Purpose Driven Church" is an excellent contemporary example of the danger of allowing heretical doctrines to be taught inside the church body.

The Danger of Deception

Sadly, many churches have suffered because of the infiltration of this subtle, evil teaching. It is interesting to also note that Rick Warren and Richard Land (former President of the Southern Baptist Convention) are both members of the Council on Foreign Relations (CFR). Started by the Rockefellers, the CFR is an organization that "inspires" and shapes many facets of the global agenda. This pride-filled organization is widely purported to have been one of the driving forces behind the United Nations, UNESCO, The IMF, The World Bank, The World Council of Churches (WCC), and The European Union. Associations with this group are also found in world conflicts, persecutions and the co-opting of churches for earthly gain. It is not surprising that even non-Christians call the CFR a sinister group. Many (if not all) of the 5,000 or so members are self-proclaimed humanists, occultists/Satanists, socialists, atheists and globalists. Most are also members of other "secret societies" like freemasonry or the Bilderberg Group. Notable members include: Bill Clinton, George Bush Sr. & Jr., Joe Biden, Barack Obama, Dick Cheney, Mikhail Gorbachev, Michael Bloomberg and Rupert Murdoch (owner of News Corp and "Christian" Publisher, Zondervan). An earnest Christian should share the following passage with Mr. Warren, Dr. Land, and the many that follow them:

> *Be ye not unequally yoked together with unbelievers: for what fellowship hath righteousness with unrighteousness? and what communion hath light with darkness? And what concord hath Christ with Belial? or what part hath he that believeth with an infidel? (2 Cor. 6:14-15)*

Be a Discerner

The heart-breaking truth is that true Christians should probably apply these verses to themselves in order to separate from the *grievous wolves in sheep's clothing* "placed" in leadership positions. Dear Believer, the body of Christ must do a better job at possessing spiritual discernment by being "wise as serpents" (Matt 10:16) and avoiding those "that by good words and fair speeches deceive the hearts of the simple" (Rom 16:18).

The Dangers of Materialism

Other manifestations of pride come through the way man attains and handles material riches, possessions, prominence and position. A portion from King David's wonderful Psalm 49 perfectly illustrates the truth. David humbly utters,

> *"They that trust in their wealth, and boast themselves in the multitude of their riches; None of them can by any means redeem his brother, nor give to God a ransom for him: (For the redemption of their soul is precious, and it ceaseth for ever:) That he should still live for ever, and not see corruption." (Psa. 49:6-9)*

David is saying that all of man's great worldly wealth, and its boasting, cannot redeem his soul nor his brother's. The Bible clearly testifies that only Christ's atoning death, as a ransom for sin, can redeem souls from eternal damnation! Other material wealth displays come from trusting in riches and worldly protections (Prov. 18:11; 1 Tim. 6:17-18), enclosing oneself in fat/prosperity (Psa. 17:10), transgressing with wine (Hab. 2:5) and being filled with the food and things of life (Hos. 13:6). Things are so good materially that they boast of tomorrow (Prov. 27:1), of their deceitful business dealings (Prov. 20:14) and of their evil doings in general (Psa. 94:4). As reviewed earlier, they are not concerned with spiritual and eternal things. The right here and now is all that matters. Deceived, these individuals believe that their success actually comes from them. One cannot forget that some of their boastfulness also comes from the positional admiration they receive from others (Jude 1:16). This last manifestation certainly spans any profession or industry. Pilots who fly large aircrafts; engineers that design large buildings; doctors that save lives; statisticians that know the truth behind numbers; politicians that appropriate funds; sales executives with millions of dollars in sales; Red Cross and homeless shelter volunteers aiding the needy; social workers helping abused children; pastors saving souls and seminary students studying God's Words, are equally disposed. God, again through wealthy Solomon, warns against accumulated affluence that is not being used to further His kingdom.

> *Riches profit not in the day of wrath: but righteousness deliffereth from death. (Prov. 11:4)*

> *There is a sore evil which I have seen under the sun, namely, riches kept for the owners thereof to their hurt. (Eccl. 5:13)*

Fleshly and Lustful Pride

Closely linked to materialism is fleshly and lustful pride. The Bible plainly asserts that these individuals walk after their own lusts (Jude 1:16) which leads to fornication and adultery (Deut. 22:24-29; Ezek. 22:10-11). They also cannot satisfy their enlarged desire (Hab. 2:5) and as such become covetous (2 Tim. 3:2). Once firmly in this sin bondage, they will want to keep "like-minded" sinners in their midst (1 Cor. 5:2). They even bless their evil-doer friends (Psa. 10:3) and consequently despise those that are good (2 Tim. 3:3). Not only does this give them a "friend" to scheme with, but also makes them feel okay about what they are doing. There are no "do-gooders" around to make them feel "uncomfortable." Because of their fleshly iniquities they do not mourn sin (1 Cor. 5:2).

Body Language and Pride

The Eyes

One of the most obvious manifestations of pride comes from "Body Language." *While not always one hundred percent accurate, these bodily displays often depict that pride is alive and well in the individual.* As with the other manifestations, Scriptures outline several physical cues to this external haughtiness. First addressing the eyes, while giving His "Sermon on the Mount," our Lord and Savior Jesus Christ said,

> *"The light of the body is the eye: if therefore thine eye be single, thy whole body shall be full of light. But if thine eye be evil, thy whole body shall be full of darkness. If therefore the light that is in thee be darkness, how great is that darkness!" (Matt. 6:22-23)*

It is noteworthy that under the influence of pride, the eyes create darkness within man.

Next, the Scriptures speak of "lofty eyes" in Isaiah 5:15 which connotes a look of haughtiness and self-absorption. This is often exhibited in movies, television and print advertisements. Many have achieved temporal worldly success using this Satanic snare. Because of this perceived success, it is then mimicked by the world as the "cool" or even the "financially prudent" thing to do. While it may look seductive...it is evil personified.

The other prideful display associated with eyes is called by the Bible, wanton eyes (Isa. 3:16). Wanton eyes are essentially eyes that are unrestrained, reckless and/or lustful. They showcase a desire to see things that should not be seen. It becomes the "lust of the eyes" written about in First John 2:16. It does not look away from things that are inappropriate to view. The record of Noah and Ham is a "picture-imperfect" illustration. In Genesis 9:20-25, Ham views (does not look away or hide his eyes) Noah's nakedness and is subsequently cursed, along with his progeny. It is a direct connection with eye wantonness and its aftermath. The Holy Canon cites, *"For we walk by faith, not by sight:"* (2 Cor. 5:7). While this portion of Scripture is not a direct parallel to the discussion, it exemplifies the spiritual truth that what one takes-in through the eyes is not always beneficial. Closely associated with the truth of lofty and wanton eyes is a proud countenance. (Psa. 10:4). Here the "whole" face is displaying proud features. The mouth, cheeks and eyes, and for some, the ears and nose may play a prominent role in this demonstration.

The Neck

Moving a few inches down from the eyes, one sees that pride similarly displays itself in the neck. In Nehemiah 9:16, the faithful recorder of God's Words, and governor, writes to captive Israelites about their ancestor's behaviors: "that they dealt proudly and hardened their necks." This "neck hardening" implies someone who is stubborn and rigid as they will not look up or down or to either side. This is mostly accompanied by un-Biblical beliefs and opinions, although not always. These individuals are immovable in the sense that no other point of view is even worth considering. In like fashion, the Bible also cites of "walking with stretched forth necks" (Isa. 3:16). This second neck indicator suggests loftiness; a mindset of superiority. They want to see all and be seen by all. It is a manifestation closely aligned with having a "high look" (Psa. 101:5; Prov. 6:17; 21:4).

The Shoulder

Moving slightly down again a couple of inches, the Bible points out that the shoulder also plays a role in displaying pride. The "withdrawn shoulder" (Neh. 9:29) originally showed how oxen would not submit to the yoke of the plough. For people, it showcases obstinate pride in the form of literally turning from someone as they are speaking to you. It can also be an indicator of not desiring fellowship with an individual. Likewise, it is the antithesis of repentance, which is the complete turning of the body to go in a righteous direction. In the end, it indeed indicates a lack of submission.

The Body

Before leaving the topic of pride's bodily manifestations, it would be advisable to meditate on two passages that exemplify how one should treat our God-given bodies.

> Let not sin therefore reign in your mortal body, that ye should obey it in the lusts thereof. (Rom. 6:12)

> What? know ye not that your body is the temple of the Holy Ghost which is in you, which ye have of God, and ye are not your own? For ye are bought with a price: therefore glorify God in your body, and in your spirit, which are God's. (1 Cor. 6:19-20)

The body presents a living testimony, to a world living in darkness, of what God has done in a believer's life.

The Mind, Heart, and Pride

Another way that pride manifests itself is through the mind and heart. Meditating on worldly wisdom, the Apostle Paul states,

> "For the wisdom of this world is foolishness with God. For it is written, He taketh the wise in their own craftiness." (1 Cor. 3:19)

Probing deeper, the Words of God declare that the proud are highminded (2 Tim. 3:4), possess a fleshly mind (Col. 2:18), are unteachable (John 9:34) and therefore scorn instruction (Prov. 13:1). They may also possess worldly, religious or even Bible knowledge (1 Cor. 8:1) but even with much "knowledge" they will teach doctrines contrary to godliness (1 Tim. 6:1-4). Often inexperienced in leadership roles (1 Tim. 3:6), they will behave proudly against elders (Isa. 3:5; 1 Cor. 1:10-13) be disobedient to parents (Rom 1:30; 2 Tim. 3:2) and will look at other's sins first and greater than their own (Luke 18:9-14). Searching the heart, the earnest Christian must never forget the following:

The heart is deceitful above all things, and desperately wicked: who can know it? (Jer. 17:9)

Another solemn warning that all should heed is:

Beware when you feel you have arrived! Beware when you feel you are very important and that God could not get along without you! Beware when you start to rob God of the glory that belongs only to Him.[39]

The Proud and Truth

How do the proud relate to displays of truth? According to the Scriptures, not very well. The Bible says that the proud are destitute of truth (1 Tim. 6:5) and resist the truth (2 Tim.3:8). People who either live in sin or believe that they know all the truths of the universe fall into this category. Not shockingly, since they know no absolute truth, they are trucebreakers (2 Tim. 3:3) and traitors (2 Tim 3:4). Being absent of truth allows them to create snares/traps (Jer. 43:2; Psa. 119:51, 85) and to easily invent evil things (Rom. 1:30) often in quiet/alone moments (Psa. 36:4). They will frequently lie to protect their "perfect" reputations. Fittingly, the Bible also declares that the proud have no substance (Prov. 25:14).

---

[39] Warren Wiersbe, <u>The Strategy of Satan</u> (Carol Stream, IL: Tyndale House Publishers, 1979), 61.

Pride Creates a Tense Environment

Prideful people will also create a tense environment wherever they go. When you get several proud people together the atmosphere often becomes combustible. Unfortunately, this is all too common in today's "civilized" society. The Bible clearly avows that contention *only* comes by pride (Prov. 13:10; 1 Cor. 1:11). Other evidences of tense surroundings come when the proud stir up strife and envy (Prov. 28:25; Rom 1:30), are scornful and wrathful (Prov. 21:24), are fierce (2 Tim. 3:3), have a history of violence (Psa. 73:6; 86:14) and display willful and domineering actions (2 Tim 3:4). The proud also exhibit incontinence (2 Tim. 3:3), recklessness (Isa. 3:16), brawling (Tit. 3:2) and drunkenness (Isa 28:1-3). After the fight there will be the flight (Hab. 2:5) and they will, in due course, permanently separate themselves from others (Prov. 18:1).

Pride and Self-Seeking Interests

Pride also manifests itself in self-seeking interests.

For all seek their own, not the things which are Jesus Christ's. (Phil. 2:21)

It seeks hobbies, amusements, distractions and games above the reading of God's Words or fellowshipping with the brethren. The puffed-up seek their own interests and not those of others because they are conceited (Prov. 26:12) and lovers of their own selves (2 Tim. 3:2). Often flattering self (Psa. 36:2), the proud are always concerned with external appearances (e.g. Scribes and Pharisees in Matt. 23:24-28), bringing attention to oneself (Isa. 3:16-17) and pleasing crowds (Gal. 1:10). Clothing and hair are frequently the tool of choice in getting attention (1 Pet. 3:3). All told, as discussed earlier, the proud will compare themselves to others (Luke 18:11).

Pride and Charity

Another major set of pride's manifestations is headed by not having charity (love in action) for others (1 Cor. 13:4). Equally, the proud will not show nor desire much natural affection (2 Tim. 3:3). Over the last generations, there has been a dramatic and observable decline in charity and affection. Surely, most people receive affection from close relatives but how about neighbors, coworkers or plain strangers? Tragically, it has become almost non-existent. Why? It is in part because of the sin of pride.

Pride and Rejection

More and more, people are afraid of rejection, afraid to give off false signals, and afraid of being sued. This environment of fear and mistrust is driven by a hostile media and government that is serving Satan's interests. An even more disturbing demonstration of pride has been the increase of rejoicing at the misery of others (Oba. 1:12). This is more than just being numb to death and suffering. It is the enjoyment of it. What is to be expected from a world that more and more celebrates abortion and euthanasia?

Pride and Other Bad Character Traits

It is worth noting that the prideful will look out only for their own things (Phil. 2:4), are idle (Ezek. 16:49) and lazy (Prov. 26:16). Paradoxically, the combination of these three manifestations can only lead to greed and covetousness. Likewise, covetousness can extend to persecuting the poor (Psa. 10:2) in order to extract even greater gain. This is frequently demonstrated by a lack of extending mercy to others (Matt. 18:28-30). Other displays of the self-absorbed are that they will oppress others (Psa. 119:122), show contempt for others (Psa. 123:4), deal wickedly without cause (Psa. 119:78; 140:8), convey ungratefulness or ingratitude (2 Tim. 3:2; 2 Chron. 32:25) and blame others, as did the first parents in the garden (Gen. 3:12-13).

The Subtlety of Pride

As mentioned previously, pride is often very subtle. It can be so subtle that the sinner may be in a deluded state of denial. Because of this some may believe that they are happy (Mal. 3:15) or will imagine things (Luke 1:51). Others will simply deceive themselves and be conceited while doing it (Prov. 28:11).

> *For if a man think himself to be something, when he is nothing, he deceiveth himself. (Gal. 6:3)*

In Paul's first chapter to the Romans, the proud and boastful form part of an exhaustive list that illustrates the interconnectedness of all of those sins.

Below is a concise listing of pride's manifestations:

> Arrogance; self-promotion; lack of giving to God and others; a selfish attitude; don't need anyone else; refusal to listen to the advice of others; a spirit of rebellion; bragging; a lack of humble regard for God and others; inability to receive a compliment; need to reach certain levels in life; life revolves around our motives, talents, gifts and desires; not asking for help; desire to be number one or first; continual reference to oneself; desire to be the center of attention. Will dress, walk, talk to get attention; need to seek praise and compliments; a need to be in prominent places or with prominent people; unwilling to help less fortunate; a rebellious nature; taking credit for others work; refusal to do menial tasks; refusal to apologize when wrong; attitude of self-sufficiency.[40]

To be supplemented with a more inclusive list of pride's modern displays:[41]

1. Complaining against or passing judgment on God. (Num. 14:1-4, 9, 11; Rom. 9:20)

---

[40] Charles Stanley, <u>Landmines in the Path of the Believer</u> (Nashville, TN: Thomas Nelson, 2007), 21-22.

[41] Stuart Scott, <u>From Pride to Humility: A Biblical Perspective</u> (Bemidji, MN: Focus Publishing Incorporated, 2010), 6-10.

2. A lack of gratitude in general. (2 Chr. 32:25)
3. Anger - Outbursts, withdrawing, pouting or frustration. (Matt. 20:1-16)
4. Seeing yourself as better than others. (Luke 7:36-50)
5. Having a falsely inflated view of your importance, gifts and abilities. (1 Cor. 4:7)
6. Focusing on lack of gifts and abilities. Always focusing on themselves. Self-pity is pride. (1 Cor. 12:14-25)
7. Perfectionism often for recognition or to feel good about themselves. (Matt. 23:24-28)
8. Talking too much. (Gal. 6:3)
9. Talking too much about yourself. (Prov. 10:19)
10. Seeking independence or control. Being under authority is a problem. (1 Cor. 1:10-13; Eph. 5:21)
11. Being consumed with what others think. (Gal. 1:10)
12. Being hurt or angered by criticism. Easily offended. (Prov. 13:1)
13. Unteachable. (Prov. 19:20; John 9:13-34)
14. Being sarcastic, hurtful or degrading. (Prov. 12:18;12:23)
15. A lack of service. (Gal 5:13)
16. A lack of compassion. (Matt. 5:7)
17. Being defensive or blame shifting. (Gen. 3:12-13)
18. Not admitting when you are wrong. (Prov. 10:17)
19. A lack of asking forgiveness. (Matt. 5:23-24)
20. A lack of Biblical prayer. (Luke 18:10-14)
21. Resisting authority or being disrespectful. (1 Pet. 2:13-17)
22. Minimizing your own sin and shortcomings. (Matt. 7:3-5)
23. Maximizing others sin. (Matt. 7:3-5)
24. Being impatient or irritable with others. (Eph. 4:31-32)
25. Being jealous or envious. (1 Cor. 13:4)
26. Using others for gain. (Matt 7:12; Phil. 2:3-4)

27. Deceitfully covering up sin, faults and mistakes. (Prov. 28:13)
28. Using attention getting tactics. (1 Pet. 3:3-4)
29. Not having close relationships. Either because of contention or through self-sufficiency. (Prov. 18:1)

Rounding out the list is a few extra-Biblical, but yet practical, quotes on pride's manifestations. No doubt, a great number can personally identify with some of the statements.

"Listening is difficult for people who think they are special (i.e. proud)."[42]

"Prideful individuals think only about how they can benefit from a relationship."[43]

"People with insecurities want to be noticed for the work that they do."[44]

"Pride never admits failure and over-emphasizes self."[45]

Sadly, *pride also looks down on others trapped in sin and entices us to favor people who say flattering things about us.*

Pride: the Foundational Evil

The ultimate point on pride's demonstrations is that *man cannot get to any other sin without first passing through the sin of pride*. Said differently, blasphemy, theft, covetousness, adultery, idolatry, lying, murder, and dishonoring parents are not possible without the foundational evil of pride. Further expanding the argument, it is not just the Ten Commandments that have to pass through pride. Every sin that is committed, whether spiritual

---

[42] Gary Fenton, <u>Good for Goodness' Sake: 7 Values for Cultivating Authentic Character in Midlife</u> (Birmingham, AL: New Hope, Pub. 2006), 186.

[43] Charles Stanley, <u>Landmines in the Path of the Believer</u> (Nashville, TN: Thomas Nelson, 2007), 29.

[44] Ibid., 26.

[45] Ibid., 16.

or physical, has pride at its root. Some may doubt and quote from First Timothy 6:10 stating that the root is really the "love of money."

> *For the love of money is the root of all evil: which while some coveted after, they have erred from the faith, and pierced themselves through with many sorrows.*

Pride and Money

While not taking away from the horrible evils of "loving money," believers should consider the complete counsel of Scripture on the matter. Satan does not love money. He really does not need it. He can pretty much get most of what he wants for free! Adam and Eve did not love money. God had already given them everything! God never called "the love of money" an abomination, but He called pride an abomination. God never said "the love of money" comes before destruction, but He said pride does. The reality is that you need the heinousness of pride before "loving" money!

In closing this section, here are two quotations exemplifying the above argument.

> "Pride is the inherent sin of man, and yet it is of all sins the most foolish. A thousand arguments might be used to show its absurdity; but none of these would be sufficient to quench its vitality."[46]

> "Pride is the epidemic vice. It is everywhere and manifests itself in many ways...Pride is the beginning of every sin."[47]

If you read this last section and rightly determined that many of pride's displays permeate much of your life, then God's Spirit has convicted your heart. Through the

---

[46] Charles Haddon Spurgeon.
http://www.Spurgeon.us/mind_and_heart/quotes/p4.htm#pride (accessed October 3, 2011).

[47] Stuart Scott, <u>From Pride to Humility: A Biblical Perspective</u> (Bemidji, MN: Focus Publishing Incorporated, 2010), 5.

power of God's Words, there may be more conviction as the study now moves onward to explore the wicked "TLM."

CHAPTER 7

THE TONGUE, LIPS & MOUTH (TLM)

The most audible and sometimes most sinister of all of pride's displays proceed from a slight non-vital organ called the tongue. Found within a small orifice called the mouth and surrounded by the lips, these three combine to form a poisonous team. Three passages aptly illustrate their venomous toxicity and ubiquity.

First, James (half-brother of Jesus Christ) pens that as the TLM goes so does the rest of the body.

> *For in many things we offend all. If any man offend not in word, the same is a perfect man, and able also to bridle the whole body. (Jas. 3:2)*

Second, our Lord and Savior Jesus Christ spoke about the mouth's connection to the heart. In Matthew's Gospel, He says,

> *"O generation of vipers, how can ye, being evil, speak good things? for out of the abundance of the heart the mouth speaketh." (12:34)*

Lastly, James again succinctly described the tongue's lethality:

> *Even so the tongue is a little member, and boasteth great things. Behold, how great a matter a little fire kindleth! And the tongue is a fire, a world of iniquity: so is the tongue among our members, that it defileth the whole body, and setteth on fire the course of nature; and it is set on fire of hell. (Jas. 3:5-6)*

TLM and the Heart

Just from these passages, one can correctly ascertain that while evil and iniquity are housed in the heart, they only need to travel ten inches or so to inflict their deadly destruction. But why does this happen? Author Joseph Stowell gives part of the answer. He stresses,

"Our proneness to elevate ourselves over others often stimulates negative speech."[48]

Criticism of Others to Elevate Themselves

Anyone who has read any small part of the Canon of Scripture has learned about individuals who have used their God-given mouth to enact verbal evil on others in order to elevate themselves. Their thinking was always rather shortsighted as the Scriptures show how their evil eventually "boomeranged" within their lifetimes.

Judgment Based Upon Your Words

In addition to the worldly ramifications of pride, one must never forget that part of the eternal end-times judgment rests on the words one chooses to communicate by:

For by thy words thou shalt be justified, and by thy words thou shalt be condemned. (Matt. 12:37)

(Many of pride's consequences will be explored in subsequent sections).

Checking Scripture with Scripture, it is also undeniably true that eternal salvation comes from verbally professing the heart-felt belief in Christ's sovereign deity (Matt. 10:32; Rom. 10:9; 1 John 4:3).

Pride and Words

Looking at pride's verbal manifestations, God's Words state that sin is typically accompanied by a multitude of words (Prov. 10:19). These words can be either foolish proclamations (Prov. 12:23; 26:5), hasty vows, as found with Jephthah the Judge (Jdg. 11:35), or vain and empty words (2 Pet. 2:18; Jude 1:16). Expanding on the concept, there is a natural connection between vain words and exaggeration. Exaggeration is basically another form of lying as it seeks to manipulate and control others. Nebuchadnezzar exaggerated in Daniel 3:19 by demanding

---

[48] Joseph Stowell, <u>Tongue in Check</u> (Wheaton, IL: Victor Books, 1983), 35.

that "the furnace be turned seven times hotter." Often accompanied by boasting, there is no substance in exaggeration.

Pride and Flattery

Closely tied with exaggeration is another form of spoken pride called flattery. *In flattery, the ultimate goals are: attention, reciprocated compliments, seduction into immorality and favor-gaining*. The Bible describes flatterers as "men pleasers" in a negative sense. Essentially, it is a smooth and subtle form of deceit. Flattery desires to gain control. Thus, it is inextricably linked with pride (Psa. 12). The following two verses best describe the connection:

> *For there is no faithfulness in their mouth; their inward part is very wickedness; their throat is an open sepulchre; they flatter with their tongue. (Psa. 5:9);*

> *A man that flattereth his neighbour spreadeth a net for his feet. (Prov. 29:5)*

Pride and Integrity

There is also often a lack of integrity associated with proud speech since it is regularly connected to lying (Psa. 59:12; 119:69), speaking evil of others (Tit. 3:2), declaring grievous and contemptuous things against the righteous (Psa. 31:18), falsely accusing (2 Tim. 3:3), and making slanderous comments (Rom. 1:30). With this last manifestation, strong mention is made that slander is a tool of revenge. Lastly, while seeming counter-intuitive, the Bible illustrates that yelling or screaming is not necessary for speech to be evil. Much of evil speaking (if not all) can be accomplished through soft tones and whispers (Rom. 1:29).

Pride Alienates

Contention

TLM accomplishes its greatest destruction as it boastfully offends and alienates others. These grievances are realized through mocking and deriding (Psa. 119:51; 140:5), debating (Rom. 1:29), asking questions that lead to strife (1 Tim. 6:4) and complaining/murmurings (Num. 14:1-4, 11; Matt. 20:10-12; Jude 1:16). Murmuring is essentially having a critical spirit that protests and nurses a damaging attitude toward the people involved and/or the situation encountered. It is always about not receiving what one thinks he deserves; perceiving that his "rights" have been violated. It is always driven by fear or lack of trusting in God. It is also regularly accompanied by the traits of self-pity, anger, impatience and irritation.

Negative Speech

Looking at verbal pride from a different perspective, one notes that it is directly connected to negative speech patterns in Scripture. Two of these speech patterns are: perverse speech (Prov. 8:13) and reviling the Lord (Psa. 10). Pride is also solidly linked with slander of the righteous (Psa. 59) as well as with scoffing and oppressive threats (Psa. 73:6-11). Peninnah (Elkanah's lead wife) verbally provoked barren Hannah to tears and poor eating (1 Sam. 1:6-7). When Samuel was born, Elkanah humbly affirmed Hannah's vow and his desire that God would establish every word that was to come out of Samuel's mouth. In fulfillment of the vow, Samuel would not injure others with vain or proud words.

Pride and Prophecy

If only all Christians would have this level of grace the world would be a very different place. Unfortunately, only those who believe in Scripturally problematic "Post-Millennialism" or "Dominion Theology" would assume that the world will once again become a paradise prior to our Lord's return. The Bible clearly prophesies increased apostasy and decreased natural affection. If it were not so, why would Christ need to return if man can create utopia all by himself?

Pride, Gossip, and Backbiting

Voiced pride is also synonymous with gossip and backbiting (Rom 1:29-30; 2 Cor. 12:20). The desire for being the center of attention is often the reason for this type of sin. Pride is fed from having information that no one else possesses and is satisfied because others (engaged in gossip) intently listen.

> *A talebearer revealeth secrets: but he that is of a faithful spirit concealeth the matter. (Prov. 11:13)*

It is interesting to note that almost everyone will readily admit to being hurt by gossip and false accusations but rarely, if ever, will anyone confess to being guilty of it. It goes back to pride's treacherous nature!

Pride and Unwholesome Speech

In addition, the haughty boldly speak shameless and impudent things (Psa. 94:4). There is no temperance as they are consumed in unwholesome speech (1 Tim 3:6) which can take the form of either cursing or coarse humor. And finally, the tongue continues to be the most expedient device to exalt oneself. This is accomplished through its boastings (Rom 1:30; 2 Tim. 3:5), self-praise (Prov. 27:2), and arrogance (1 Samuel 2:3; Isa. 13:11).

Concluding Remarks Concerning TLM

In concluding this subject of the evil triumvirate of the TLM, one sees that in Hannah's prayer, the Lord commands not to let pride and arrogancy come out of the mouth:

> *Talk no more so exceeding proudly; let not arrogancy come out of your mouth: for the LORD is a God of knowledge, and by him actions are weighed. (1 Sam. 2:3)*

In addition, the Apostle Peter, quoting from David's 34th Psalm, admonishes saints to refrain from spoken evils. Cephas writes,

> *"For he that will love life, and see good days, let him refrain his tongue from evil, and his lips that they speak no guile: Let him eschew evil, and do good; let him seek peace, and ensue it." (1 Pet. 3:10-11)*

In conclusion, Paul also has something valuable to say about this very subject. He writes to the Ephesians,

"Let no corrupt communication proceed out of your mouth, but that which is good to the use of edifying, that it may minister grace unto the hearers." (Eph. 4:29)

What Our Prayer Should Be

Dear Heavenly Father, please help us refrain from evil talk. Purge it from our hearts. Guide us in having graceful speech. Let us provide a pleasing testimony to the unbeliever. Allow us to build-up and minister to the saints in our midst. In the Name of Jesus Christ. Amen.

CHAPTER 8

EXAMPLES OF PRIDE AND ITS CONSEQUENCES

In The Garden

As explored in the introduction, the world's first example of pride is found with Satan or the Devil. Some of his other Biblical names are Serpent, Dragon, Beelzebub, Belial, Wicked One and Prince of the Power of the Air. Also considered was the first act of pride in humanity with Adam and Eve. Shortly after that first act or the "fall of man," consequences came in rapid succession. Initially, Adam and Eve felt shame as they realized their nakedness (Gen. 3:7), soon to be followed by fear and the eventual hiding of themselves in the trees (Gen. 3:8). The feeling of shame must have been powerful because of the self-delusion of trying to hide from an Omnipotent Creator God as if He could not find them amongst the trees. Adam then shifted blame to God and Eve (Gen. 3:12), while Eve accordingly blamed the serpent (Gen. 3:13). (It is curious to note that proud/haughty people find it very difficult to accept responsibility for their actions. Humanity has definitely inherited this horrible trait from its first ancestors!) Then God cursed all three players in the act:

> *And the LORD God said unto the serpent, Because thou hast done this, thou art cursed above all cattle, and above every beast of the field; upon thy belly shalt thou go, and dust shalt thou eat all the days of thy life: And I will put enmity between thee and the woman, and between thy seed and her seed; it shall bruise thy head, and thou shalt bruise his heel. Unto the woman he said, I will greatly multiply thy sorrow and thy conception; in sorrow thou shalt bring forth children; and thy desire shall be to thy husband, and he shall rule over thee. And unto Adam he said, Because thou hast hearkened unto the voice of thy wife, and hast eaten of the tree, of which I commanded thee, saying, Thou shalt not eat of it:*

cursed is the ground for thy sake; in sorrow shalt thou eat of it all the days of thy life; Thorns also and thistles shall it bring forth to thee; and thou shalt eat the herb of the field; In the sweat of thy face shalt thou eat bread, till thou return unto the ground; for out of it wast thou taken: for dust thou art, and unto dust shalt thou return. (Gen. 3:14-19)

Humankind has been paying the consequences ever since this moment. Nevertheless, Christians know from Scripture that God is just and righteous and that Satan will eventually experience the ultimate consequence. He will be cast into the lake of fire for eternity after being loosed toward the end of Christ's Millennial Reign (Rev. 20:10)!

After the Garden

Surveying post-Edenic portions of God's Words, one comes across numerous examples of pride, haughtiness and self-exaltation. The first one to be explored is the pride of Cain. Cain's pride started "innocently" enough through his laziness as his offering from the ground was not respected by God (Gen. 4:4). Immediately after experiencing God's rejection, his pride began to pick-up steam as he became wroth, soon to be followed by his falling countenance. Cain's pride then became even more pronounced as he did not listen to God's loving advice and strong caution. *"If thou doest well, shalt thou not be accepted? and if thou doest not well, sin lieth at the door. And unto thee shall be his desire, and thou shalt rule over him."* (Gen. 4:7) Instead of listening to God's instruction, Cain took his sinful pride further and slew his brother (Gen. 4:8). Next, he lied to God by denying knowledge of his brother's whereabouts followed by disrespectful language. *"And the LORD said unto Cain, Where is Abel thy brother? And he said, I know not: Am I my brother's keeper?"* (Gen. 4:9) From the rest of the account, one reads of Cain's shame, the proclaimed consequences, and the Creator's ultimate protection to the transgressor. From this brief section, one can plainly glean that pride seems to initially present itself in "harmless" fashion, such that most people would ignore its occurrence.

However, if not controlled, pride quickly begins to overwhelm more important aspects of one's life until complete destruction occurs. *With Cain, pride went from laziness to anger to dejection to not listening to killing to lying and to insolence.* Similar patterns of pride's damaging infiltration are evidenced throughout God's inspired Words!

Pride Precipitates the Universal Flood

About 1,480 years and three Genesis chapters later, one finds that God's Spirit would no longer strive with man. Why? The Bible declares that evil hubris and malevolence had completely encompassed mankind.

> *And GOD saw that the wickedness of man was great in the earth, and that every imagination of the thoughts of his heart was only evil continually. (Gen. 6:5);*
>
> *And God looked upon the earth, and, behold, it was corrupt; for all flesh had corrupted his way upon the earth. (Gen. 6:12)*

God's Patience...Then Judgment

Even with immorality engulfing mankind, God begins showing one of His eternal virtues; His longsuffering. Not wanting to completely decimate the whole earth, God gives mankind one hundred twenty more years to repent. God also finds a "perfect" man (named Noah) whom He could use to save the land animals, birds and the human race. Noah was not only used to build the ark, he was also used in those pre-flood years to warn others of the impending catastrophe.

Sadly, his generation was ungodly and surely filled with prideful self-absorption. Other than Noah's family, no one else was worthy to be lifted-up above the flood destruction. Peter's Second Epistle proclaims,

> *"And spared not the old world, but saved Noah the eighth person, a preacher of righteousness, bringing in the flood upon the world of the ungodly." (2 Pet. 2:5)*

(For Biblicists, the "lifting-up" and salvation of Noah is a type of the pre-tribulation "rapture" comprised of born-again believers of the universal church. [1 Thes. 4:13-18; Rev. 3:10]).

What followed was a cataclysmic, worldwide flood that for a short period cleansed the world of unrighteousness and changed its topography to this day.

Pride Surfaces Again

Only a few hundred years later, man again was up to universal no-good exclusively driven by baseless pride. Set in ancient Babylonia, the local dwellers provide one of the most haughty statements found in the Bible:

> *And they said, Go to, let us build us a city and a tower, whose top may reach unto heaven; and let us make us a name, lest we be scattered abroad upon the face of the whole earth. And the LORD came down to see the city and the tower, which the children of men builded. (Gen. 11:4-5)*

Analyzing the verses, pride's fingerprints are identified throughout. First, one notes that the people wanted to feed their so-called egos by building a great tower that would touch the sky. It is nothing less than Satan's familiar theme of desiring to "exalt their throne above the stars of God," "ascend into the clouds," and "be like the most high." They also knew that this feat would give them notoriety and position to feed their already growing arrogance. Most importantly and what is not normally taught is that the inhabitants were acting in explicit disobedience to God's command to multiply and replenish the earth by wanting to stay in one location (Gen. 9:1). The direct result was that God confused their languages and scattered them across the earth. *"Therefore is the name of it called Babel; because the LORD did there confound the language of all the earth: and from thence did the LORD scatter them abroad upon the face of all the earth."* (Gen. 11:9) Given God's directive, it is interesting to observe what is occurring today.

Many Cities Today Are Like Biblical Cities

Is it a coincidence that some of the most despicable acts of pride and haughtiness are committed in the largest and most famous cities across the globe? Cities such as New York, Los Angeles, Miami, San Francisco, Las Vegas, Vancouver, Rio de Janiero, Paris, Geneva, London, Amsterdam, Bangkok, Calcutta, Hong Kong etc., always seem to display the worst of man. The hate of God, the lewdness, the materialism and the disregard for life all seem to be viler and coarser in these metropolises. People incorrectly believe that they can more effectively hide their sin amongst the multitude. Most conservative Bible-believing churches in these cities were also hijacked by Satan, making it very difficult for someone to truly hear the Gospel of salvation as well as receive spiritual "meat" for growth and maturity. Followers should earnestly pray that the Lord raise up Godly leaders to do His work in these dens of iniquity. It's worth noting that in addition to ancient Babylon, the Bible mentions numerous other evil and prideful cities. Some of the cities mentioned are: Sodom, Gomorrah, Nineveh, Neo-Babylonia, Tyre, Sidon, Alexandria, Samaria, Damascus, and even, Jerusalem.

Pride and Bible Personalities

Ahab

Approximately 1,300 years later (long after Abraham, Isaac, Jacob, King David and the dividing of Israel), readers come across the Bible's "dynamic duo" of pride; Samaria's King Ahab and his equally-yoked Jezebel. The Scriptures state,

> *"But there was none like unto Ahab, which did sell himself to work wickedness in the sight of the LORD, whom Jezebel his wife stirred up." (1 Kgs. 21:25)*

The son of Omri, Ahab reigned a total of twenty-two drama-filled years. From the start, Ahab was erecting altars and building groves to the false god, Baal, for his own personal worship. He likewise did not follow the commandments (18:18) and did more (through his evil) to provoke the Lord than any king before him (16:29). The Bible informs us that, through the prophet Elijah, the Lord punished Israel for Ahab's evil doings with a three-year drought. As expected, Ahab also built urban centers and even constructed an opulent house of ivory (22:39). (PETA and other environmental extremists would exact a good portion of revenge today.)

As examined earlier, fear always comes from an unhealthy concern for self. This is precisely what Ahab demonstrated when he did not deny Syrian King Benhadad's demand for Ahab's wives, children, gold and silver (20:7). Showing cowardly pride, Ahab did not act until his princes shamed him into leading his army into battle (20:14). After achieving military victory, he was again guilty of pride through the false humility of releasing King Benhahad. Like Joshua, the Judges, and King Saul many years before, Ahab did not obey the Lord's command to utterly destroy the idolatrous enemy. Through a prophet, Ahab was given his judgment:

> *And he said unto him, Thus saith the LORD, Because thou hast let go out of thy hand a man whom I appointed to utter destruction, therefore thy life shall go for his life, and thy people for his people. (1 Kgs. 20:42)*

In proud fashion, Ahab did not repent of his sin, but instead simply returned to Samaria displeased.

Jezebel

Turning to Jezebel, the Holy Words show that she was responsible for adversely stirring the heart of Ahab and slaying many Godly prophets of Israel. Ironically, she sought to exact her vengeance by killing Elijah the prophet for his slaying of 450 satanic prophets of Baal (1 Kgs. 19:2). These deceitful prophets likely ate at Jezebel's table because they "tickled" her ears with deceits. Truth was not important to her due to her vanity and haughtiness. As noted previously, evil people desire to be surrounded by like-minded individuals in order to ease their guilt and avoid repentance, even if they are being lied to. The Bible also declares that Jezebel was involved in many witchcrafts and spiritual whoredoms (2 Kgs. 9:30).

The Sordid Tale of Naboth, Ahab, and Jezebel

One of the most sordid tales of pride and deception occurs in First Kings 21. It starts when Ahab becomes dejected because of his failure to purchase a much desired vineyard from a subject named Naboth. (Here again Ahab is consumed with self.) The record progresses as Jezebel enacts a Machiavellian scheme to possess the vineyard; a scheme that only could have been birthed by Beelzebub himself. She first proclaims a day of fasting to deceitfully honor Naboth. Once Naboth was exalted, Jezebel contracts two men of Satanic-Belial worship to bear false witness. These false witnesses slandered Naboth by proclaiming that he had blasphemed God and the king. Spectacularly lifted and then torn down publicly, Jezebel could now have Naboth stoned to death, taking ownership of the land, and subsequently gift it to Ahab. Many Christian historians refer to the fact that similar demonic schemes have continued throughout "modern" history, citing the accounts of the Lusitania, Pearl Harbor and for some, "September 11th."

As prophesied, Ahab's life ends paradoxically as he was killed (while in fearful disguise) by the army whose King he so "diplomatically" released not long before. A few years later, Jezebel was unceremoniously thrown from a high window, resulting in her death. In the end, both served as nutrition for dogs. Paul's writing to Timothy appropriately describes the account of Ahab and Jezebel and many others throughout history: *"But they that will be rich fall into temptation and a snare, and into many foolish and hurtful lusts, which drown men in destruction and perdition."* (1 Tim. 6:9)

Uzziah

Less than 100 years later and 50 or so miles south, another example of pride comes from Uzziah, King of Judah and son of Amaziah. Uzziah became king at sixteen and reigned for fifty-two years. His reign coincided with the reign of Jeroboam II in Israel and the prophetic ministries of Jonah, Amos and Hosea. The Scriptures state that Uzziah initially did what was right and sought the Lord and was prospered (2 Chron. 26:5). Several years into his reign, when he became strong, his heart was lifted through pride. He began to believe that he was the one responsible for his wealth, power and long rule. Uzziah subsequently disobeyed God's command by burning incense in the temple (2 Chron. 26:16), which was something that was decreed by God only to be done by the priests. Even after being rebuked by Azariah the priest, Uzziah's pride made him steadfast in his unrepentance and wrath. To his amazement, the results were disastrous. Uzziah contracted leprosy and was cut off from the Lord's house for the rest of his life. In further humiliation, while still living, he lost his reign to his son, Jotham (2 Chron. 26:18-21).

Naaman and Gehazi

The next example of pride comes from the chronicle of Naaman, a Syrian captain who was desperately seeking to unearth a cure for his leprosy. Naaman's wife had a Samaritan maid who informed her of a God-led prophet who could cure Naaman of his leprosy. Naaman, now motivated, received permission from the King of Syria and packed his clothing, gold, and silver. Arriving in Israel with his company and chariots, Naaman presented himself to King Jehoram and subsequently traveled to meet Elisha. All appeared to be going well until he was met by Elisha's servant, Gehazi. Naaman may have thought, "Does Elisha not know my stature and prominence by not meeting me himself?" Adding "insult to injury," the messenger instructed Naaman to go wash in the less than pristine Jordan River seven times! Here is Naaman's response:

> *Are not Abana and Pharpar, rivers of Damascus, better than all the waters of Israel? may I not wash in them, and be clean? So he turned and went away in a rage. (2 Kgs. 5:12)*

Naaman came all that distance and was yet consumed by so much pride that he could not even comply with simple instructions in order to get cured. Ironically, in today's medical world, one often observes this very dynamic. People want immediate cures for their ailments without humbling themselves or sacrificing their unhealthy lifestyles. "Please make me lose weight and lower my cholesterol so I can still eat cheese, bacon, and fries." "Please control my diabetes as long as I can eat my daily donut." "Give me a vaccine that can help me prevent HPV so that I can continue having sex whenever and with whomever I want." Returning to Naaman, the good news is that once he tamed his haughtiness, he bathed himself seven times and was miraculously healed. In summation, this passage beautifully illustrates how earnest disciples need to humble themselves and trust The Lord in order to receive the blessings He has in store for them!

Haman

A most intriguing example of pride comes from Haman the Agagite. In the book of Esther, one learns that Ahasuerus (King of Persia) gave Haman a seat of standing above all other princes (Est. 3:1). As expected, all of the king's servants bowed and revered him, with the exception of a Jewish scribe named Mordecai (3:2). When Haman saw that Mordecai did not bow or revere him, the Words of God assert that Haman became full of wrath (3:5). He initially wanted to punish Mordecai but rather thought it best to completely destroy the whole Jewish race (3:6). Haman's pride then moved him to start devising an evil scheme by giving King Ahasuerus misleading information and manipulating the king's greed through the presentation of potential financial gain. The episode reads:

> *And Haman said unto king Ahasuerus, There is a certain people scattered abroad and dispersed among the people in all the provinces of thy kingdom; and their laws are diverse from all people; neither keep they the king's laws: therefore it is not for the king's profit to suffer them. If it please the king, let it be written that they may be destroyed: and I will pay ten thousand talents of silver to the hands of those that have the charge of the business, to bring it into the king's treasuries. (Esth. 3:8-9)*

The king approved and decreed a day whereby all Jews (young, old, women and children) could be destroyed, killed or caused to perish. The end result being that their spoil would be confiscated (3:13). As evil pride always takes satisfaction in the misery of others, one also reads about Haman having a drink, perhaps in early celebration (3:15). Later in the account, Queen Esther becomes involved as she invites Haman and the king to a private banquet with the sole purpose of protecting the Jews. Not knowing Esther's intentions, Haman's heart fills with prideful joy that even Mordecai's not bowing was insufficient to ruin his grand moment. Immediately, Haman goes home to boast exceedingly about all of his feats:

> *And Haman told them of the glory of his riches, and the multitude of his children, and all the things wherein the king had promoted him, and how he had advanced him above the princes and servants of the king. Haman said moreover, Yea, Esther the queen did let no man come in with the king unto the banquet that she had prepared but myself; and to morrow am I invited unto her also with the king. (Esth. 5:11-12)*

In being liable for possibly the most boastful statement in the Bible, it is accurate to say that Haman was overflowing with self-love. (Take note parents: placing children above God and obedience is a sinister form of pride!) Even still, he knew that all would not be complete until Mordecai was hung in the gallows prepared for the occasion by Haman (5:13). Lest the brethren forget that pride's desire is never quenched!

Prior to the private banquet, an interesting interlude occurs in the account. Because of his desire to impress the king, Haman gets humbled as he must honor his hated enemy (Mordecai) in a manner that he artfully recommended for "another" honoree (6:6-13). Shortly thereafter, one reads of Haman's final act of pride as he crudely positions himself on the bed next to Queen Esther, this after being accused of trying to murder the Jews (7:1-8).

In summary, here are Haman's exhibitions of pride. He became wrathful and vengeful when he did not get the reverence he thought he deserved. This led him to exact evil calculations on the Jews that included manipulating the king and others for their destruction. It is significant that Haman was also satisfied with the planned infliction of pain and suffering on others, was ecstatic to be part of the "in crowd," made many arrogant statements, and positioned himself seductively with the Queen in the very shadow of the king. One is relieved to know that the record ends justly, with Haman losing his house and ring, and with his hanging on the very gallows meant for Mordecai. As will be examined later, pride's consequences can take many forms; one of them is being humbled!

Diotrephes

Moving to the New Testament, one finds perhaps the most obscure but yet one of the more disturbing examples of pride. It deals with a church leader named Diotrephes. Only mentioned once in Scripture, the Apostle John indicts him in his third epistle. John writes:

> *I wrote unto the church: but Diotrephes, who loveth to have the preeminence among them, receiveth us not. Wherefore, if I come, I will remember his deeds which he doeth, prating against us with malicious words: and not content therewith, neither doth he himself receive the brethren, and forbiddeth them that would, and casteth them out of the church. Beloved, follow not that which is evil, but that which is good. He that doeth good is of God: but he that doeth evil hath not seen God. (3 John. 1:9-11)*

John names names with Diotrephes, a leader who wants to be considered first among men. He rules the church with an iron fist likely because he does not want to be exposed for what he really is; an ungodly leader. Diotrephes' pride forbids receiving anyone who does not share his viewpoint. Not only that, but he goes as far as to not allow those of the congregation to receive them. He is even willing to cast out and risk the spiritual life of his "sheep" in order to keep his standing and control. Although not called such, Diotrephes is a strong candidate for being considered a false brother/teacher. At the risk of psychologizing, it also appears that John's intimate relation with Christ and his knowledge of the Scriptures creates insecurity in Diotrephes' mind that results in defensiveness. His pride even prompts him to speak malicious words against John. Just think, if Diotrephes can speak evil of an apostle like John, then no one is safe from this type of slanderous heart. So-called church leaders like Diotrephes are what prompted Christ to warn believers, some years before John's letter, *"Beware of false prophets, which come to you in sheep's clothing, but inwardly they are ravening wolves"* (Matt. 7:15).

Pride and Secular Personalities

Bishop Eddie Long

The final example of haughtiness is set in today's world. It provides obvious evidence of pride to outsiders (ironically not so much to insiders) along with the forewarned sad results. In 2010, Bishop Eddie Long, who was then the senior pastor of the 25,000 member, New Birth Missionary Baptist Church near Atlanta, Georgia, faced civil suits from four young men that indicted him on sexual coercion charges. A year or so later, it was reported by the *Atlanta Journal-Constitution* that the lawsuits were settled out-of-court with undisclosed terms.[49] Just recently, another lawsuit was filed indicting Mr. Long on charges concerning his involvement with a third party company (called by plaintiffs a Ponzi scheme) that defrauded congregants. While the guilt or innocence has yet to be determined on this second series of allegations, it appears that pride was well entrenched in this ministry long before its current fall. In 2005, while the *Atlanta Journal-Constitution* was initially investigating Mr. Long's $1.4 million home, his salary of over

---

[49] Shelia M. Poole, "Eddie Long Case Officially Dismissed". *Atlanta Journal-Constitution,* May 27, 2011.

$250,000 a year and the use of a $350,000 Bentley, Mr. Long responded in the following manner:

> We're not just a church; we're an international corporation. We're not just a bumbling bunch of preachers who can't talk and all we're doing is baptizing babies. I deal with the White House. I deal with Tony Blair. I deal with presidents around this world. I pastor a multimillion-dollar congregation. You've got to put me on a different scale than the little Black preacher sitting over there [who's] supposed to be just getting by because the people are suffering.[50]

Apart from the egregious Biblical error of baptizing babies (which is a man-made doctrine never mentioned in Scripture!), it is quite possibly one of the most narcissistic statements ever given from a so-called man of God. It is unbelievable that people would actually stay in that church after that statement was made.

An additional warning bell is Mr. Long's relationship with Tony Blair. Mr. Blair (Former UK Prime Minister and Founder of "The Tony Blair Faith Foundation") is an avowed ecumenist and Fabian Socialist. For many, his discreet goal is to create false unity in order to co-opt the church for the purposes of setting up the "One-World Church" and the "One-World Government." Please pray for Mr. Long to find true humility and repentance, and to separate from un-regenerates like Tony Blair. Also pray for his congregation to establish a church where its leaders possess Christ-like humility. As of this writing, amid his wife filing for divorce, and many fittingly asking him to step down as Pastor, Mr. Long finally consented to a hiatus. Still short of a complete resignation, it represents a step in the right direction. *"But there were false prophets also among the people, even as there shall be false teachers among you, who privily shall bring in damnable heresies, even denying the Lord that bought them, and bring upon themselves swift destruction"* (2 Pet. 2:1).

---

[50] Eugene Robinson, "Pride Goeth Before the Headlines," *Ebony Magazine,* December/November 2011.

Celebrity Worship

In conclusion, if you are one of the many that partake in Satan's menu of pop culture offerings (television, movies, magazines, sundry amusements etc.) you will be barraged with images and statements from people who are lovers of self and pleasure (2 Tim. 3:2-4). Through the "worship" of celebrity, Christians and non-Christians are exposed to all forms of narcissism, sexual depravity, boastfulness and open hostility toward the Holy Creator God. Tragically, a form of flattery, through mindless imitation, has permeated and negatively influenced the willingly ignorant world. This is what the Apostle John warned about when he wrote about not loving the things of the world (1 John 2:15-17). For that reason, this study will not bestow additional "air-time" to the countless examples of actors, singers, athletes, writers and other public figures that through actions, words and beliefs have become instruments of Satan. Knowingly or not, they have subtly, and many times blatantly, propagated everything that God abhors. *"For without are dogs, and sorcerers, and whoremongers, and murderers, and idolaters, and whosoever loveth and maketh a lie"* (Rev. 22:15).

CHAPTER 9

CONSEQUENCES OF PRIDE

The Words of God are exhaustive regarding pride's consequences. These consequences range from those that impact human relationships to ones that produce eternal separation from God in fiery hell. The analysis below will attempt to capture many of them.

The first grouping can be best associated with God's initial responses to the sin of pride as the Bible testifies that God will discover their secret parts (Isa. 3:17). This speaks to the truth that nothing (even sins of the spirit) can be done without God's knowledge.

Both Peter and James indistinguishably voice that God will resist the proud (Jas. 4:6; 1 Pet. 5:5). How alarming it should be to anyone to have the Omnipotent God against you. Needless to say your life will not amount to much being resisted by the Almighty God! On a positive note, it is great to note how much unity of heart and mind was shared by the teachings of the apostles and the early church.

The Scriptures then state that God will rebuke and curse the proud (Psa. 119:21), will hide His goodness from them (Psa. 31:19-20) and will know them only at a distance (Psa. 138:6). The full verse in Psalms declares,

> *"Though the LORD be high, yet hath he respect unto the lowly: but the proud he knoweth afar off."*

A deeper exposition denotes that personal intimacy will be absent since God's presence in the lives of the proud will be distant. Prayers are hindered. Scripture understanding is clouded. The blessings that God wants to bestow upon His creation are essentially forsaken.

The Bible also conveys that God will not suffer the proud (Psa. 101:5) and will potentially remove them (Ezek. 16:50; Zeph. 3:11). What a terrifying list of consequences.

Just this small list should be enough to dissuade a Christian from pride or turn an unbeliever to Christ. The reality is that these initial consequences are only the beginning.

The Judgments of God Are Coming

The ensuing set of consequences expresses that God will weigh every single action of man (1 Sam. 2:3). This weighing of actions will occur during either the Judgment Seat of Christ, reserved for saved believers (Rom. 14:10; 2 Cor. 5:10), or the Great White Throne Judgment that is set aside for those who did not truly believe in Christ (Rev. 20:11-15).

Regarding after-life consequences for born-again believers that exhibit pride, the Scriptures only offer a few glimpses. The Gospel of Matthew testifies,

> *"But it shall not be so among you: but whosoever will be great among you, let him be your minister; And whosoever will be chief among you, let him be your servant." (20:26-27)*

The Gospel of Mark offers two separate accounts:

> *And he sat down, and called the twelve, and saith unto them, If any man desire to be first, the same shall be last of all, and servant of all. (9:35)*

> *But so shall it not be among you: but whosoever will be great among you, shall be your minister: And whosoever of you will be the chiefest, shall be servant of all. (10:44)*

In all three cases, the eternal consequences of pride for the saint are clear; they will be the least in the kingdom and will serve others. Regardless, one can be certain that the works done in the millennial kingdom will be joyous since they will occur in the holy presence of Lord Jesus.

The Eternal Consequences for the Unbeliever

If the proud never believed in Christ, their eternal consequences are very different from those of believers. God's Words declare that they will be plentifully punished by God (Psa. 31:23; Prov. 16:5), and thereby will receive the same condemnation as Satan (1 Tim. 3:6). After the rapture, the proud unbeliever could burn in the Tribulation and be stubble, if there is no repentance and turning to Christ (Mal. 4:1). The Bible also says that they will descend to hell (Isa. 5:14), provoke the wrath of God (2 Chron. 32:26), experience God's anger (Job 9:13), suffer destruction (Prov. 15:25; 16:18), and will be confounded (Psa. 97:7). This last Psalm states, *"Confounded be all they that serve graven images, that boast themselves of idols: worship him, all ye gods."* This verse undeniably states how pride and boasting in idols will confuse the individual. In America, one sees this type of idolatry most prevalent in Roman Catholicism and Mormonism (it is also present in other "Christian" denominations and false cults) where statues, beads and other relics become part of the worship experience.

Believers or Unbelievers?

Some could very well have an earnest heart-belief in Christ but will infuse pagan veneration into true Biblical devotion. The line between the two is often blurred, creating a dangerous spiritual condition where at best, there is no Heavenly power, or at worst, demonic powers could be invoked. For many, eternal salvation is gravely at risk especially if their trust, beliefs and prayers are focused on images created by man.

Since both believers and non-believers engage in the sin of pride, the truth is that they will both be subject to the following humiliations in life. They will be brought down by God (2 Samuel 22:28; Isa. 25:11; 26:5), bowed down by God (Isa. 2:11, 17; 13:11), and will be humbled and abased (Job 40:11; Psa. 106:43; Isa. 2:11; 5:15; 10:33; Ezek. 21:26; Daniel 4:37; Matt. 23:12; Luke 14:11; 18:14). The Holy Bible also cites that the proud will stumble and fall (Prov. 16:18; Jer. 50:32), be brought low (1 Samuel 2:7; Job 40:12; Proverbs 29:23; Isa. 3:5; 13:11; 25:5; Jas. 1:9), will suffer shame (Prov. 11:2; Psa. 119:78), have their lips put to silence (Psa. 31:18), have less hope than a fool (Prov. 26:12) and live with a spirit of anger (Eccl. 7:8). If the world truly meditated only on this above list, they would be foolish not to ask God to remove this heinously destructive sin from their life.

Some of pride's aftermath regarding doctrine and sin are as follows: They are reprobate (rejected) concerning faith (2 Tim. 3:8), they believe and propagate false doctrine (1 Tim. 6:3-4), and will be defiled (Mark 7:23). Through their demonic charisma they will lead silly women into sin (2 Tim. 3:6), and, in general, allure others into sin and wantonness.

> *For when they speak great swelling words of vanity, they allure through the lusts of the flesh, through much wantonness, those that were clean escaped from them who live in error. (2 Pet. 2:18)*

Pride, Thoughts, and Imagination

Pride also has consequences on how people think and absorb information. The Canon of Scripture testifies that the mind will be hardened (Dan 5:20) and corrupted (1 Tim. 6:5; 2 Tim. 3:8). Truth is often blocked out by this sort of mindset. It would then stand to reason that oneself is deceived (Prov. 28:11; Jer. 49:16; Obad. 1:3), and though ever learning, never coming to the knowledge of the truth (2 Tim 3:7). How many brilliant P.h.D.'s ignore/reject the blatant inconsistencies and lies of the "Big Bang" and "Darwinian Evolutionary" theories that do not escape the mind of an average eight year old! Accordingly, the proud will not listen (Job 35:12; Jer. 13:15) and will be scattered in their own imagination (Luke 1:51). This last verse in Luke is intriguing because in today's usage, imagination is a positive word, very much like pride was identified earlier as a positive word. However, in thirty-five of the thirty-six uses in the King James Bible, the words imagine(d), imagineth and imagination have negative connotations. They speak of the proud being driven by their deceitful hearts rather than by the Spirit of God. One must remember that "creative" imaginations, without God's leading, will lead man away from abiding in God through Jesus Christ.

Pride and Relationships

Man's pride and boasting also severely disturb relations with others. Initially, their folly will be manifested unto all men (2 Tim. 3:9) and they will not be respected by the righteous (Psa. 40:4) who will eventually withdraw from them (1 Tim. 6:5; 2 Tim. 3:5). In turn, the proud will mistrust Godly men (Jer. 43:2) and will have perverse disputings. They will also possess envy and strife (1 Tim. 6:4-5) that will lead to division, (John 7:34; 10:19; 1 Cor. 1:10; 3:3), making others cry (Job 35:12) and weep (Jer. 13:17). Ironically, while others around them cry, they will not mourn themselves (1 Cor. 5:2). It stands to reason that they will not have close relationships or fellowship with others (Prov. 18:1; Heb. 10:25) and eventually will be cut off from among his people (Num. 15:30-31). Lastly, strangers will take their strength (Hos 7:9) while others will conspire against them (2 Chron. 33:24). These consequences should not be surprising since God's Words unequivocally state:

> *He is proud, knowing nothing, but doting about questions and strifes of words, whereof cometh envy, strife, railings, evil surmisings, perverse disputings of men of corrupt minds, and destitute of the truth, supposing that gain is godliness: from such withdraw thyself. (1 Tim. 6:4-5).*

Author Wayne Mack offers a supplementary perspective on how pride impacts relationships and usefulness in the church age. He writes:

> "One of the consequences of pride is an uncontrolled tongue that lashes out at others. Proud people hurt other people because they are slanderous, gossiping, quarrelsome and divisive. They alienate people and destroy relationships. Another consequence of pride is being unteachable. Proud people are stubborn and therefore they remain spiritually immature. Further, pride leads to dishonesty and inconsistency. Proud people cannot be trusted because they do not value the

commitments they have made to others. Ultimately, pride robs people of joy, peace and usefulness for Christ."[51]

Along the same lines, Super Bowl winning football coach Tony Dungy writes,

"Over time, blowing your own horn ends up backfiring and chipping away at any respect you might think you deserve."[52]

Pride and Descendants

The results of pride are also felt by the holder's descendants. The Scriptures provide an excellent example of how children will suffer as a result of their parent's pride. Remember "evil" King Ahab? First Kings proclaims how his late act of repentance gave him a stay of execution on the consequences stemming from his prideful behavior. What happened to the consequences? They were passed on to his son, Joram: *"Seest thou how Ahab humbleth himself before me? because he humbleth himself before me, I will not bring the evil in his days: but in his son's days will I bring the evil upon his house."* (1 Kgs. 21:29) Although not deterministic, this verse conclusively demonstrates that sometimes sins are felt generationally. The Bible is replete with instances of haughtiness taught or passed down by fathers to their sons. Amon, son of Manasseh (2 Chr. 33:23-24), Rehoboam, son of Solomon (1 Kgs. 12:4-14), and Belshazzar, son of Nebuchadnezzar (Dan 5:30) are but a few examples.

Pride and a Difficult Life

The last group of pride's Biblical consequences relate to a very difficult life here on earth. This truth applies even to the saved individual. This is so because repenting of your sins, believing/professing that Jesus Christ is the Son of God, believing that He rose from the dead and is now at the right hand of the Father, atones you of your sins and

---

[51] Wayne Mack, <u>Humility: The Forgotten Virtue</u> (Phillipsburg, NJ: P&R Publishing, 2005), 90.

[52] Tony Dungy, <u>Uncommon</u> (Carol Stream, IL: Tyndale House 2009), 22.

sanctifies you to be in the presence of God. However, it does not remove the earthly consequences of your sins. God's Words state that the proud will languish/become weak (Isa. 24:4), be trampled/tread upon (Isa. 28:1-3), be oppressed, suffer affliction, experience sorrow (Psa. 107:39), and likely undergo famine (Zeph. 2:9-11). More than likely, the affliction and sorrows will make the proud age ungracefully (Eccl. 12:4). Lastly, the proud will not prosper:

He that covereth his sins shall not prosper: but whoso confesseth and forsaketh them shall have mercy. (Prov. 28:13)

Undoubtedly, pride will create emotional, physical, and mental misery. How much more does one need to hear before realizing that pride will eventually make life much more problematic and steal the joy of abiding in Christ?

Pride and a Personal Intimate Relationship With God

The final and most important result of pride, one that should gravely concern every unsaved person, is that

"Pride prevents us from experiencing a personal, intimate relationship with the Savior...Pride literally erects an emotional wall between the Savior and us."[53]

What results for the unbeliever is that the Gospel is perceived as foolishness.

But the natural man receiveth not the things of the Spirit of God: for they are foolishness unto him: neither can he know them, because they are spiritually discerned. (1 Cor. 2:14)

For the believer who is still fully embracing pride, the result is carnality and stunted maturity. Very little spiritual growth is experienced (1 Cor. 3:3; Eph. 4:15).

This concludes the examination on the displays and devastations of pride in the life and afterlife of individuals. These manifestations and consequences, however, do not

---

[53] Ibid., 36.

just apply to people, as some mistakenly believe. They also apply to nations. The Bible gives several such illustrations as will now be explored.

CHAPTER 10

PRIDE AND NATIONS

As just stated, the displays and aftermaths of hubris are not just limited to individuals, but also relate to nations. The Scriptures are rich in examples. Much of it was fascinatingly penned as unfulfilled prophecy at the time it was written, proving the additional point that literal prophecies have literal fulfillments.

Bible Nations

Israel

To gain understanding of this Biblical truth, one must first study God's chosen nation, Israel (and Judah). (Both titles will be used interchangeably unless Scripture warrants a difference.) God initially warns Israel that He will mar them because of their pride (Jer. 3:9). They will work in vain and their land will not yield increase (Lev. 26:19-20). Israel and Judah then received God's judgment for their pride (Isa. 29:4) and were consequently doomed because of it (Jer. 13:18). As punishment for their pride and haughtiness, God then raised up adversaries (Isa. 8:7; 9:11; Lam. 1:17; Amos 3:11 that humbled their men (Isa. 2:9) and brought them low (Deut. 28:43; 2 Chron. 28:19). Their prideful iniquity had some of them even taken into captivity (Jer. 13:9, 17; Hosea 5:5) while others were made to wander and suffer hunger (Deut. 8:2-3). Only a few were able to stay in Judah as caretakers while the rest were simply killed. In Ezekiel 16, Judah's pride was shockingly compared to Sodom's:

> *As I live, saith the Lord GOD, Sodom thy sister hath not done, she nor her daughters, as thou hast done, thou and thy daughters. Behold, this was the iniquity of thy sister Sodom, pride, fulness of bread, and abundance of idleness was in her and in her daughters, neither did she strengthen the hand of the poor and needy. And they were haughty, and committed abomination before me:*

therefore I took them away as I saw good. (Ezek. 16:48-50)

Even the "Daughters of Zion' were smitten because of pride (Isa. 3:16-17). Two other passages condemning Israel's pride are: The tribe of Ephraim behaving like a silly dove without a heart (Hos. 7:11) and the tribe of Benjamin being humbled (almost eliminated) due to the rape and murder of a concubine (Jdg. 19:24). This passage will be studied more closely in a later chapter. Just think, had they been completely annihilated, the world would not have had the fourteen Epistles from Saint Paul, a Benjamite!

Other Biblical Nations

Israel was not the only country that was guilty of pride. The Bible declares that Egypt was taken down because of it (Exod. 10:3; 18:11; Ezek. 30:6), eventually resulting in the departing of their scepter. (Zech. 10:11). God's Words also state that He cut off the pride of the Philistines (Zech. 9:6), brought down Assyria because of their pride (Zech. 10:11), and that the pride of Babylon will be recompensed (Jer. 50:29-32). Finally, Moab was found to be exceedingly proud as they displayed loftiness, arrogance and haughtiness (Isa 16:6; Jer. 48:29), and were correspondingly punished by God. The Almighty also told Moab that their lies would cease (Isa. 16:6). This prophecy has already been fulfilled since they have long stopped being a nation.

Post-Modern Nations

The "Post Modern" world is eerily reminiscent of the ancient Greek and Roman cultures. Like western culture of today, their cultures exalted pride and belittled humility. Make no mistake, just as their arrogance and haughtiness greatly contributed to their demise, it will contribute and hasten the fall of modern society. The self-destructiveness of rampant pride makes this an inescapable fact. Every civilization relies on reciprocally supportive relationships among its people for well-being. Thus, it stands to reason that when great numbers of individuals become primarily dedicated to the goal of self, society disintegrates. Modern society is experiencing this in every aspect of life. Greater division and strife is observable in areas of work (increasing hostility and mediation among employees), enterprise (growing fraud and unethical tactics), politics (intensifying malicious personal attacks), sports (rising levels of anger for players and fanatics) and education (increased blurring of truth and sexualization). In all of those cases, pride, resulting in greed and envy have practically incapacitated growth and productivity. Even in some churches, more than a few believe that they somehow have tapped into God's secret knowledge in ways that few others have experienced.

Another common theme between all of these nations (extinct or current) can be best summed up by the following quote:

> "All wars between nations, all selfishness, all suffering, all ambitions, all jealousies and all embittered lives with daily unhappiness are the result of the root sin of pride."[54]

This is a truly sobering statement for the major countries of the world (United States included).

Revival is Needed

Nations should take note of these Biblical consequences and start re-building the foundation of their governments on the shoulders of Jesus Christ (Isa. 9:6) and His corresponding humility. Only then will a spiritual revival take place. Revivals have occurred throughout the history of the world as they did during Israel's occupation of the "Promised Land." Brethren should fervently pray to God to deliver revival if it is His will. If it happens, then all should praise God, since many more souls would be delivered from endless fire and anguish, and prosperity and peace would be extended for a time. *"For the transgression of a land many are the princes thereof: but by a man of understanding and*

---

[54] Andrew Murray, <u>Humility</u> (New Kensington, PA: Whitaker, 1982), 24.

knowledge the state thereof shall be prolonged." (Prov. 28:2) However, as one reads from the Canon of Scripture (and as past experience here on earth has shown), revivals are relatively short-lived and are typically followed by even greater periods of rebellion and apostasy. The unfortunate reality is that mankind will never experience a perfect theocracy until Christ's Thousand Years is established.

Lost Man's Need

Dear Reader. If you have read this far and are not certain where you would spend eternity, why would you not want to settle the matter with God? Life without a close, loving and certain relationship with Christ and the Father is at best challenging and at worst painful and difficult. God created you for worship; to worship Him. He never wanted you to be in pain and suffering without His comfort. Jesus said,

> *"Come unto me, all ye that labour and are heavy laden, and I will give you rest. Take my yoke upon you, and learn of me; for I am meek and lowly in heart: and ye shall find rest unto your souls. For my yoke is easy, and my burden is light." (Matt. 11:28-30).*

Always seek God while he is near. The steps to Him are so simple. First, admit that you are a sinner. *"For all have sinned and fall short of the glory of God."* (Rom. 3:23). Second, acknowledge that the consequence of sin is eternal separation from God in an excruciating place through the many consequences just explored. Third, repent of your sins so much so that you no longer want to engage in them. If you have done these first three steps, then please read the following passage: *"That if thou shalt confess with thy mouth the Lord Jesus, and shalt believe in thine heart that God hath raised him from the dead, thou shalt be saved. For with the heart man believeth unto righteousness; and with the mouth confession is made unto salvation."* (Rom. 10:9-10). If you have professed Christ with your mouth and believed in your heart that God raised Jesus Christ from the dead, then you are now a child of God. Born-again, sanctified, justified, and never to be separated from Him!

Now live for Christ and abide in Christ. Seek Him throughout the day in prayer. Yearn to read His Words daily. Desire to be in the company of other believers in the worship of God.

The Christian's Need

Dear Christian. You believe and have professed Christ but may not have completely submitted all aspects of your life to the Lord and Saviour. You may not pray or read God's Words as often as you once did. Financial or health worries may be gripping you. As a result, your joy and peace is sporadic. Your worship may, at times, feel empty, distracted and powerless. Relationships are still a struggle. Doubts of sundry kinds may be entering your mind. Why? You may have held on to some of the world's activities and have rationalized them as "liberty." There may be unforgiveness that you are harboring. You may even be battling a sin habit that seems insurmountable. Do not despair. The Bible says:

> Be careful for nothing; but in every thing by prayer and supplication with thanksgiving let your requests be made known unto God. And the peace of God, which passeth all understanding, shall keep your hearts and minds through Christ Jesus. (Phil. 4:6-7)

Rededicate your life to Christ. Submit everything you have to Him. God can keep you from your pride (Job 33:17). Make yourselve low and die daily in Christ. True joy comes from complete humble submission to Him. Fittingly, the study now moves to learning about what God's Words say about humility and meekness.

CHAPTER 11

EVIDENCES AND MANIFESTATIONS OF HUMILITY

The lovely evidences of humility and lowliness are found throughout Holy Scripture. Believers are blessed, not only to have an opportunity to read them, but to have them as models to follow. Our prayer should be that our daily walk be cloaked by these wonderful traits as illustrated by this beautiful Andrew Murray quote:

> The insignificances of daily life are the tests of eternity because they prove what spirit really possesses us. It is in our most unguarded moments that we really show and see what we are. To know the humble man, to know how the humble man really behaves, you must follow him in the common course of daily life.[55]

Characteristics of the Humble

As established previously, a humble and lowly man will seek the Lord's face in times of abundance or affliction. (2 Chron. 7:14; 33:12; Psa. 142:6; Zeph. 2:3). The saint will delight in a close relationship with our Lord Jesus Christ as he looks unto Him (Heb. 12:2) and lives for Him (Phil. 1:21). In harmony with his relationship with Christ, he will have fear of the Lord (Prov. 22:4; Rom. 11:20-21; Eph. 5:21), tremble at God's Words (Isa. 66:2), and rely on God for judgment and knowledge (Psa.19:66). A truly humble man never forgets what God has done for him (Deut. 6:10-12), feels unworthy to question God (Rom. 9:19-23) and believes dying is gain (Phil. 1:21). Ultimately, he realizes that *"Humility begins with recognizing you are not God."*[56]

---

[55] Andrew Murray, <u>Humility</u> (New Kensington, PA: Whitaker, 1982), 57.
[56] Gary Fenton, <u>Good for Goodness' Sake: 7 Values for Cultivating Authentic Character in Midlife</u> (Birmingham AL: New Hope Pub., 2006), 178.

Through this closeness with God, the humble will pray (2 Chron. 7:14; Luke 18:13), pray without ceasing (1 Thess. 5:17), pray for others (2 Tim 2:1-2), confess sins (1 John 1:9), remember past affliction/misery (Lament. 3:19-20) and feel contrition (Isa. 57:15). It is remarkable to note that even though the humble will remember past afflictions and have contrition for those acts, they will be transformed by the renewing of the mind (Rom. 12:2). How powerful to remember past wrongs but yet be renewed. Only a Holy God can perform that miracle!

Humility and Worship

Humility is also manifested in how the believer prepares for proper worship (2 Chron. 30:11). As such, they will fast to get closer to God (Psa. 35:13), will serve the Lord before and after the service (Acts 20:19), and joyfully receive the Words of God (Jas. 1:21). The humble saint will offer God anything for the grace He has received (Psa. 116:12-19), will look unto Jesus (Heb. 12:2), and as examined earlier, will boast in a Holy God (Psa. 44:8).

Humility and the Mind

The Holy Bible makes a captivating connection between humility and the mind. The Holy Spirit, through Luke and Paul, gives two verses affirming this truth. They are:

> *Serving the Lord with all humility of mind, and with many tears, and temptations, which befell me by the lying in wait of the Jews. (Acts. 20:19)*

> *Put on therefore, as the elect of God, holy and beloved, bowels of mercies, kindness, humbleness of mind, meekness, longsuffering. (Col. 3:12)*

God's Words also pronounce that the humble are sober-minded (Rom. 12:3) and will have the same mind toward one another (Rom. 12:16). They are not wise in their own conceits (Rom. 12:16) but always let others praise them instead of themselves (Prov. 27:2). The mature and earnest Christian will cloth himself daily with humility (1 Pet

5:5). Saints must remember that meekness is never an accident. It is not part of life's natural "maturing" process. It comes from a desire to have it and desire to live it through God!

> "Authentic humility is also more than a reaction to aging. It is deliberate act of the will."[57]

The Most Visible Proofs of Humility

The most visible proofs of humility are frequently expressed by relationships with each other. It was said that, *"Humility toward men will be the only real sufficient proof that our humility before God is real."*[58] Therefore, the truly meek and humble will forbear one another in love (Eph. 4:2; Col. 3:13), are longsuffering/patient (Col. 3:12), are slow to wrath (Jas. 1:19), will forgive one another (Col. 3:13), will serve one another (Gal. 5:13; Matt. 20:27), loves his brother (1 John 4:20; 1 Cor. 13:4), will have tears (Acts 20:19), will rejoice and weep with others (Rom. 12:15), and will bear each other's burdens (Gal. 6:2). The humble will also enjoy close relationships (Acts 20:31-38), will have charity towards others (1 Cor. 13:4), are concerned with other's interests (Phil. 2:4), will instruct those that oppose themselves (2 Tim. 2:25) and are tender-hearted (2 Kgs. 22:19; 2 Chron. 34:27) because they are gentle and not brawlers (Titus 3:2). The truly humble readily condescend to persons of low estate (Rom. 12:16), does not think higher of himself than reality indicates (Rom. 12:3), and esteems others greater than himself (Phil. 2:3; Rom. 12:10). The humble man is also giving and has good works (1 Tim 6:17-18), loves mercy, and accordingly acts justly (Mic. 6:8). Finally, humility manifests itself in the bewailing of un-repenting sin (2 Cor. 12:21). A lovely quote on this very theme reads,

> "Our love for God is measured by our fellowship with men and the love it displays...Humility toward men

---

[57] Gary Fenton, <u>Good for Goodness' Sake: 7 Values for Cultivating Authentic Character in Midlife</u> (Birmingham, AL: New Hope Pub., 2006), 170.

[58] Andrew Murray, <u>Humility</u> (New Kensington, PA: Whitaker, 1982), 57.

will be the only real sufficient proof that our humility before God is real."[59]

Humility also displays itself in relation to others through its willingness to submit to authority (1 Pet. 2:13-17; Rom. 13:1), be subject to brethren and elders (1 Pet 5:5), hear their father's instruction (Prov. 13:1), accept rebuke/reproof (Prov. 9:8), be teachable (Num. 22:22-35) and to unvaryingly accept punishment for iniquities (Lev 26:41). "Humility before God is nothing if not proved in humility before men."[60]

The brethren, and most definitely the unsaved, should be able to see, feel, and experience the humility that is only possible through a life-saving relationship with Jesus Christ. One must remember that true humility is not just a "state-of-mind." Humility is an action word!

Humility and Words

As with pride, humility is also conveyed through spoken words. The Bible declares that the humble live quiet and peaceable lives (2 Tim. 2:2) and have a quiet spirit (1 Pet. 3:4). It stands to reason that the meek are quick to hear/listen (Jas. 1:19), slow to speak (Jas. 1:1), and will conceal knowledge and matters (Prov. 11:13; 12:23). Humility does not coexist with gossip or slander. Scripture also attests that meekness does not manifest itself in speaking evil of men (Tit. 3:2) but in good conversation (Jas. 3:13) and edifying speech toward each other (Eph. 4:29). There will also be an openness to confess sins to God (1 John 1:9). A fitting quote illustrates these Canonical truths: "A heart that is yielded to God will eliminate rebellious, murmuring, angry, lying and slanderous words."[61]

Humility and Man's Focus

The next group of humility's manifestations is best exemplified by focusing on God rather than the up and down

---

[59] Ibid., 57.
[60] Ibid., 58.
[61] Joseph Stowell, <u>Tongue in Check</u> (Wheaton, IL: Victor Books, 1983), 85.

circumstances of life. The Words of God state that the humble neglect bodily indulgences (Col. 2:23), are content in any circumstance (Phil. 4:12), and are thankful to God for everything (1 Thess. 5:18). This contentedness and thankfulness surely applies to finances as they flee the love of money (1 Tim. 6:10-11). As did the Apostle Paul, the humble will also glory and pleasure in infirmities (2 Cor. 12:9-10). Even prosperous King Solomon knew that humility with little is much better than evil pride with much.

> *Better it is to be of an humble spirit with the lowly, than to divide the spoil with the proud. (Prov. 16:19)*

Humility and Bodily Manifestations

The last major area of lowliness to be discussed centers on bodily demonstrations. The Bible outlines three specific manifestations. They are: the lowering of the eyes, the smiting or hitting of the breast, and the crouching or bowing of the whole body. Addressing in tandem the lowering of the eyes and the beating of the chest, Luke 18 offers a clear depiction of their connection to humility and contrition.

> *And the publican, standing afar off, would not lift up so much as his eyes unto heaven, but smote upon his breast, saying, God be merciful to me a sinner. (Luke 18: 13)*

In this verse, one sees the portrayal of a low and meek publican. He is pounding his chest. He is unable to look up and make eye contact. All he desires is to repent and makes things right with God. What makes this account all the more significant is that publicans (who were tax collectors) had developed warranted reputations as rampant thieves among their own people. The Bible unquestionably links the publican vocation with sin. (Matt. 9:10-11; 11:19; 18:17; 21:31-32; Mark 2:15-16; Luke 7:34; 15:11). Their philosophy could have been best described as: "One for Caesar, one for me and one for you." Even so, it shuould be noted that throughout His ministry, Jesus Christ sought after the maligned publican. He chose and commanded Matthew the Publican to follow Him and become an Apostle. Christ additionally directed publicans only to take what was correctly due (Luke 3:12-13) and feasted with them at Matthew's house (Luke 5:29-32). Christ also reached out to Zacchaeus (a rightfully defamed publican) who ultimately repented and restored four-fold all that he had stolen from others (Luke 19:2-11).

Turning back to bodily examples of humility, Luke's Gospel describes many "pounding their breasts" shortly after Christ commended His spirit to the Father. It denotes a heaviness and sadness that was felt by many of the crucifixion witnesses.

> *And all the people that came together to that sight, beholding the things which were done, smote their breasts, and returned. (23:48)*

Society still witnesses this form of humility via media images of grief-stricken individuals trying to cope with recent tragedies.

The second demonstration of physical humility is illustrated in Psalm 10:10. It states,

> *"He croucheth, and humbleth himself, that the poor may fall by his strong ones."*

This short verse clearly indicates that crouching and humbling are linked. Also called bowing, inclining, bending, prostrating, condescending, and submitting, this manifest-tation is found hundreds of times throughout the course of Scripture. Examples include: Abraham bowing to the "Angel of the Lord" (believed by many to be a theophany of the Lord Jesus Christ) just prior to the destruction of Sodom (Gen. 18:2), and also bowing to his beloved brethren before burying his bride, Sarah (Gen. 23:7-12); Jacob and his family humbly bending before Esau (Gen. 33:3-7), and Egyptian Governor Joseph bowing to his father, Jacob (Gen. 48:12). Outside of Genesis, illustrations include: Ruth bowing to Boaz (Ruth 2:10); David bowing to Jonathan (1 Sam. 20:41) and King Saul (1 Sam. 24:8); King Saul bowing to a necromanced Samuel (1 Sam. 28:14), and the women at Christ's tomb bowing to the angels (Luke 24:5). Scriptures also teach when not bowing to authority is justified (Est. 3:2-5). In this passage, believers are instructed through Mordecai's example never to honor or venerate evil men like Haman.

Scripture confirms that bowing or inclining is a God-honoring form of reverence (Exod. 4:31; 1 Kgs. 19:18; 1 Chron. 29:20; 2 Chron. 7:3; 29:29; Neh. 8:6; Psa. 146:8) as shown by King David inclining to the Lord in humble praise (Psa. 35:14; 38:6; 57:6). Oppositely, the Bible also instructs that bowing can be used for evil. Throughout history, the Israelites bowed to idols even though they had experienced the presence of God, His many miracles, and His Words through the prophets (Num. 25:2; Jos. 23:16; Jdg. 2:17; 2 Chron. 25:14; Rom. 11:4). The Bible also tells of how the Roman soldiers mockingly "bowed the knee" to Christ after placing the "crown of thorns" on His head (Matt. 27:29).

Humility's Practical Displays

A proper conclusion to this section is provided by way of a Biblically comprehensive (but not exhaustive) list of humility's practical displays.[62]

1. Recognize and trust God's character. Thank God for even the trials. (Psa. 119:66)
2. See yourself as having no right to question or judge an Almighty and Perfect God. (Psa. 145:17)
3. Focus on Christ. (Phil. 1:21; Heb. 12:1-2)
4. Frequent Biblical prayer. (1 Thess. 5:17; 1 Tim. 2:1-2)
5. Be overwhelmed with God's undeserved grace and goodness. (Psa. 116:12-19)
6. Be thankful and grateful toward others. (1 Thess. 5:18)
7. Be gentle and patient. (Col. 3:12-14)

---

[62] Stuart Scott, <u>From Pride to Humility: A Biblical Perspective</u> (Bemidji, MN: Focus Publishing Incorporated, 2010), 18-21.

8. See yourself as no better than others. (Rom. 12:6; Eph. 3:8)
9. Have an accurate view of your gifts and abilities. (Rom. 12:3)
10. Be a good listener. (Phil. 2:3-4; Jas. 1:19)
11. Talk about others only if it is good or for their good. (Prov. 11:13)
12. Be gladly submissive and obedient to those in authority. (Rom. 13:1-2)
13. Prefer others over yourself. (Rom. 12:10)
14. Be thankful for criticism or reproof. (Prov. 27:5-6)
15. Have a teachable spirit. (Num. 22:22-35; 1 Cor. 4:7)
16. Seek to build others up. (Eph. 4:29)
17. Serve. (Gal. 5:13)
18. Be quick to admit when you are wrong. (Prov. 29:23)
19. Be quick in asking and granting forgiveness. (Col. 3:12-14)
20. Repent of sin as a way of life. (1 Tim. 4:7-9; 1 John 1:9)
21. Minimize others' sins or shortcomings in comparison to your own. (Matt. 7:3-4)
22. Be genuinely glad for others. (Rom. 12:15)
23. Possess close relationships. (Acts 20:31-38)

CHAPTER 12

BLESSINGS & REWARDS
OF HUMILITY

Now that the many daily expressions of humility have been considered, it is time to explore the many wonderful blessings associated with a meek and humble spirit.

Rewards After Resurrection

For the regenerated, sanctified, and justified believer, many of the rewards of humility occur after their bodily resurrection, in the presence of Jesus Christ in His kingdom. In this light, the Bible says that the humble born-again believer will be exalted (Matt. 23:12; Luke 1:52; 14:11; 18:14; 1 Pet. 5:6; Jas. 1:9), be chief (Matt 20:27; Luke 22:26), inherit the "new" earth (Psa. 37:11; Matt. 5:3-5), be the greatest in the kingdom of heaven (Matt. 18:4; Mark 10:43-44), dwell in high and holy places with God (Isa. 57:15), and shall live forever (Psa. 22:26). What more can anyone ask for? Just to reiterate, once someone repents of their sins and truly believes that Christ died for those very sins, they shall obtain mercy (Matt. 5:7), honor (Prov. 15:33; 18:12; 22:4; 29:23), and salvation (Job 22:29; Psa. 76:9; 149:4) which comes from having their soul saved (Jas. 1:21). *The reality is that "Without humility there can be no true repentance."[63] Thus, one can say that repentance is another recompense of humility*!

The Meek and Abased

The meek and abased will also be treated differently by a Holy Righteous Father. God will not despise them (Psa. 51:17), but will rather respect them (Psa. 138:6), remember them (Psa. 9:12), hear their desires (2 Kgs. 22:19; 2 Chron. 7:14; Psa. 10:17), help them (Psa. 116:6), hide them to

---

[63] Stuart Scott, From Pride to Humility: A Biblical Perspective (Bemidji, MN: Focus Publishing Incorporated, 2010), 23.

avoid His anger (Zeph. 2:3), defer their judgments (1 Kgs. 21:29; 2 Kgs. 22:19), defend them (Isa. 11:4; Prov. 29:23), and preserve them (Psa. 116:6).

In Psalm 136, the Hebrew elect are reminded that God did not forget them and took them from their wretched existence.

> *Who remembered us in our low estate: for his mercy endureth for ever: And hath redeemed us from our enemies: for his mercy endureth for ever. (Psa. 136:23-24)*

As such, God will be near to those with a low spirit.

> *The LORD is nigh unto them that are of a broken heart; and saveth such as be of a contrite spirit. (Psa. 34:18)*

Other Blessings of the Meek

There are several other blessings, bestowed directly by God, that result from possessing a truly meek spirit. God promises to prepare their heart (Psa. 10:17), to guide them in judgment, and to teach them His way (Psa. 25:9). God will additionally give them wisdom (Prov. 11:2; 19:20; Jas. 3:13), grace (Jas. 4:6), and make them useful in the future (Deut. 8:16). Essentially, one of the blessings from being humble is receiving a state of perpetual lowness. The Lord does it for our own good. It is something that very few think about or truly desire in their lives.

> "If our heavenly Father were to let your unhumbled spirit win a victory in His holy war, you would pilfer the crown for yourself, and meeting with a fresh enemy you would fall a victim; so that you are kept low for your own safety."[64]

Humility also has multiple rewards in life's earthly journeys. Scripture proclaims that possessing humility will help avoid evil (1 Kgs. 21:29), provide an abundance of peace (Psa. 37:11), and will provide eats and satisfaction

---

[64] Charles Haddon Spurgeon. www.spurgeon.us. http://www.spurgeon.us/mind_and_heart/quotes /h2 htm#humility (accessed January 8, 2011).

(Psa. 22:26). Proverbs 22:4 also informs that humility gifts three things: *"By humility and the fear of the LORD are riches, and honour, and life."* While certainly not proclaiming the heretical "Prosperity Only" Gospel (only health and wealth will "rain" on a believer; no persecution or affliction), God's Words unequivocally state that mature Christians that are humbly led by the Holy Spirit will experience blessings that others will not. Other rewards include experiencing a revived spirit and heart (Isa. 57:15), having gladness (Psa. 34:2; 69:32), possessing increased joy in the Lord (Isa. 29:19), and being able to rejoice in all things (Jas. 1:9). More than just outright worldly prosperity, the above Scriptures make it evident that the humble will enjoy peace in the midst of fiery trials.

Humility and Present Rewards

There are also rewards of humility that immediately and positively impact others. The humble will always give true answers for their hope in Christ (1 Pet. 3:15). The meek also will have the blessing of bringing good tidings to others (Isa. 61:1), restoring others (Gal. 6:1), assuring friendships (Prov. 6:3), possessing unity with others (Eph. 4:3), and being heard by others (Psa. 10:17; 34:2). Most amazingly, they will have the reward of leading others to repentance.

> *In meekness instructing those that oppose themselves; if God peradventure will give them repentance to the acknowledging of the truth. (2 Tim. 2:25)*

The truly humble will also feel no jealousy or envy. This is because their trust is in God, not in the world. This is summarized best by the citation:

> "The joy of a tongue that blesses others from a heart of humility, patience and love is one of the rewards of the maturing believer."[65]

A final blessing realized by the humble is their ability to boast in the Lord and not of themselves (Psa. 34:12).

---

[65] Joseph Stowell, <u>Tongue in Check</u> (Wheaton, IL: Victor Books, 1983), 125.

It should also be noted that there is an implicit symbiotic relationship between humility and faith. One cannot exist without the other. The quote,

> "We can never have more true faith than we have of true humility,"[66]

is absolutely correct. The Lord Jesus on two occasions equated faith and humility:

> *The centurion answered and said, Lord, I am not worthy that thou shouldest come under my roof: but speak the word only, and my servant shall be healed. For I am a man under authority, having soldiers under me: and I say to this man, Go, and he goeth; and to another, Come, and he cometh; and to my servant, Do this, and he doeth it. When Jesus heard it, he marvelled, and said to them that followed, Verily I say unto you, I have not found so great faith, no, not in Israel. (Matt. 8:8-10)*

> *And she said, Truth, Lord: yet the dogs eat of the crumbs which fall from their masters' table. Then Jesus answered and said unto her, O woman, great is thy faith: be it unto thee even as thou wilt. And her daughter was made whole from that very hour. (Matt. 15:27-28)*

Humility breeds faith and faith breeds humility. A similar symbiosis exists with holiness and humility. It is impossible to exhibit one without the other.

> "The holiest will always be the humblest."[67]

The Crowns

No review of humility's blessings would be complete without discussing the crowns that will be given to saints once they are judged by Jesus Christ at His Pre-Millennial Kingdom Bema Seat.

The "Crown of Glory" or the "Elder's Crown" goes to Pastors/Shepherds that disciple and lead groups of believers. First Peter 5:2-4 recites,

---

[66] Andrew Murray, <u>Humility</u> (New Kensington, PA: Whitaker, 1982), 84.
[67] Andrew Murray, <u>Humility</u> (New Kensington, PA: Whitaker, 1982), 70.

"Neither as being lords over God's heritage, but being ensamples to the flock. And when the chief Shepherd shall appear, ye shall receive a crown of glory that fadeth not away."

The "Crown of Life" or the "Martyr's Crown" is given to believers that endure trials and suffering while still loving Christ and His name (Jas. 1:12; Rev. 2:10). All Christians should be gravely aware that there are countless believers earning this precious crown in countries that are openly hostile to the Gospel. They are dying while defending the name of Jesus. Many of these restricted and/or persecuting countries are located in the Middle East (Saudi Arabia, Iraq, Syria etc.), Africa (Somalia, Libya, Sudan, Egypt etc.), and Asia (China, North Korea). Surprisingly, Christian oppression is also taking place in less commonly thought of countries such as Belarus, Colombia and Malaysia. All Christians should pray and tangibly support missionaries and suffering believers in these countries.

The "Victor's Crown" or the "Incorruptible Crown" is given to disciples that run and fight till the end of their earthly life (1 Cor. 9:24-25). It denotes a believer that presses on regardless of adversity or obstacle.

The Bible also states that believers who love and yearn for Christ's appearance will receive a "Crown of Righteousness" (2 Tim. 4:8). For these dear saints, the return of Jesus Christ permeates much of their thoughts and deeds.

The fifth and final crown is found in First Thessalonians 2:19-20:

For what is our hope, or joy, or crown of rejoicing? Are not even ye in the presence of our Lord Jesus Christ at his coming? For ye are our glory and joy.

In these verses, the brethren are told that the saved will be given a "Crown of Rejoicing" for being a "soul-winner" for Christ.

In concluding this thought concerning heavenly crowns, one cannot forget that in Revelation 4:9-10, God's Words share that heavenly saints will actually "cast the crowns at the throne" of Christ. The saints in His company will no doubt know that all good things came from Him only. It will be enough just to be in His presence!

Humility and Nations

There are also blessings associated with nations that imbibe humility. The book of Second Chronicles outlines that it is possible for a nation to humble itself as well as to experience the associated rewards. The brief examination starts by presenting a verse from Leviticus that clearly speaks of God honoring the Abrahamic Covenant after all of Israel humbles itself:

> *And that I also have walked contrary unto them, and have brought them into the land of their enemies; if then their uncircumcised hearts be humbled, and they then accept of the punishment of their iniquity. (26:41)*

The Bible also shows that God humbled Israel in the wilderness to prove them and know what was in their heart (Deut. 8:3). After a forty-year trial of purging and refining, God finally allowed the Israelites to enter into the land of promise. Equally, God today is proving and testing nations as well as believers. He does this in-part to make all aware of how much He really is needed and depended upon. Once this eternal truth is known, the believer can seek rest with the Lord. Otherwise, many will just continue in their deluded state of believing that the world simply revolves around them, or that depravity is not connected to earthly or heavenly consequences.

The Bible also utters that God will hear Israel, forgive their sins, and heal their land when they humble themselves (2 Chron. 7:14). Similarly, Second Chronicles discloses that Israel avoided God's wrath (2 Chron. 12:7, 12; 32:26) and gained deliverance through Jerusalem humbling itself (2 Chron. 32:26). The Body of Christ should pray that God will raise up humble leaders across the world. The world will then reap the blessings of a safer and healthier planet, but more importantly, thousands of souls may come to know Christ and have eternal salvation through this "extension."

Humility and the Believer

Dear Believer: Never become exalted in your current position with God. It was He who was longsuffering toward you. God patiently waited for you all of those years when you only cared about yourself, when you carelessly lived in sin and had no concern for eternal things. The unadulterated truth is that there is absolutely nothing in your life, the life of others, or in this world that you can take credit for and boast of. Why? Because it has all been given to you!

> *For who maketh thee to differ from another? and what hast thou that thou didst not receive? now if thou didst receive it, why dost thou glory, as if thou hadst not received it? (1 Cor. 4:7)*

As seen above, God's Words plainly convey that God will bless and reward the meek and humble, including both individuals and nations. With that as a foundation, the study now focuses on reviewing one last set of blessings: "The Fruit of the Spirit."

CHAPTER 13

THE FRUIT OF THE SPIRIT

Near the end of the Epistle to the Galatians, the Holy Spirit guided the Apostle Paul to pen one of the most recognizable and impactful passages in all of Scripture. Chapter 5 verses 22 to 23 read,

"But the fruit of the Spirit is love, joy, peace, longsuffering, gentleness, goodness, faith, meekness, temperance: against such there is no law." (Gal. 5:22-23)

Fruit Affected by Conditions

To many, this passage outlines the output and habits produced by individuals where the Holy Spirit does not merely dwell but is working and active. If the actual fruit from actual trees is the result/reward of many factors then likewise the "Fruit of the Spirit" is also the result/reward of several events and activities. Farmers know that to grow good, tasty apples, trees require the appropriate quantity of water and sunlight. The right ambient temperature range is needed. Too cold or too hot will not work. The trees also require the right amount of pruning, oil treatment, and insecticide spraying, all to be dispensed at the precise time of the season. If any one of these variables is skewed, it can at worst, jeopardize the whole crop, or at best, produce less than desirable fruit. Similarly, for the "true" Christian, the "Fruit of the Spirit" is affected by all of the following spiritual conditions framed as questions. How often is prayer to God invoked? Is it without ceasing? How fervent are the prayers? Is there Scripture reading and meditating? Have any verses been memorized? Is church worship to God done with all of the heart? How often is there fellowship with other believers? Is charity and love demonstrated to other believers? Are the unsaved being evangelized? Are there relationships that need humble restoration? Is there a sin habit that has not been defeated? Is the past still haunting, producing nightmares? Has all been submitted to Christ? Has God been petitioned to search the heart for evil pride? Is there a seeking to improve the areas wrought with pride or has that been simply dismissed or forgotten about? All of the above questions (and many more) are important to ask and address. If not in accordance with God and the Bible, all of them will in one way or another hinder and impede the lovely "fruit" of a Christian's testimony. But as has been explored together, if a man possesses Godly humility (with all of its manifestations) then part of the remuneration will be the possessing and the reflecting of these nine practices.

The Fruit of the Spirit

Love

Starting with the first fruit of love, Jesus instructs believers to love God with everything and to love one another. Replying to one of the tempters (who happened to be a scribal lawyer), Jesus said:

> *Thou shalt love the Lord thy God with all thy heart, and with all thy soul, and with all thy mind. This is the first and great commandment. And the second is like unto it, Thou shalt love thy neighbour as thyself. On these two commandments hang all the law and the prophets. (Matt. 22:37-40)*

But how can man love God and others? The answer lies in putting aside self-exalting pride (admitting you are a sinner), believing in Christ as the Son of God, and eventually, submitting all to Him. Thus, without the prerequisite of humility, love of God and man is impossible. This truth is further elaborated by Ephesians 4:2:

> *With all lowliness and meekness, with longsuffering, forbearing one another in love.*

Evidenced here is that one must first possess lowliness and meekness to forebear each other in love.

Joy

As with love, the second fruit, genuine joy, only comes from possessing a humble and subdued heart. The prophet Isaiah provides additional insight on this veracity:

> *The meek also shall increase their joy in the LORD, and the poor among men shall rejoice in the Holy One of Israel. (Isa. 29:19)*

The joy becomes greater when one submits. Equally with James (the half-brother of the Lord), one reads that he was so submissive that he counted falling into divers temptations as joy. James would thank God for any circumstance and use it as a means to be drawn closer to an Almighty God! *Humility then is to be joy only if there is humility first toward God and then toward man.*

Peace and Longsuffering

The next two fruits, peace and longsuffering, are also blessings that come from a subdued and humble heart. With regard to peace, the Bible shows two passages that outline this linearity. First in Psalm 37:11 God's Words say,

> *"But the meek shall inherit the earth; and shall delight themselves in the abundance of peace."*

In another well-known verse, God states that submitting to Him will bring peace in the hearts of believers:

> *Be careful for nothing; but in every thing by prayer and supplication with thanksgiving let your requests be made known unto God. And the peace of God, which passeth all understanding, shall keep your hearts and minds through Christ Jesus. (Phil. 4:6-7)*

Remember that God never promised peace in the world; He only promised peace in a submitted heart. A similar link exists between humility and the fruit of longsuffering. Ephesians 4:12 and Colossians 3 illuminate the connection:

> *Put on therefore, as the elect of God, holy and beloved, bowels of mercies, kindness, humbleness of mind, meekness, longsuffering. (Col. 3:12)*

The Rest of the Fruit

When examining the final five "fruit of the Spirit" one finds the same connection between them and humility. Earlier in the study, it was established that believers can only have as much faith as they have humility. The same can be said for gentleness, goodness, meekness and temperance. Each would no doubt require a fair amount of Godly humility before coming into "fruition." The passage that may best encapsulate this last point, is found in Peter's Second Epistle:

> *And beside this, giving all diligence, add to your faith virtue; and to virtue knowledge; And to knowledge temperance; and to temperance patience; and to patience godliness; And to godliness brotherly kindness; and to brotherly kindness charity. For if these things be in you, and abound, they make you that ye shall neither be barren nor unfruitful in the knowledge of our Lord Jesus Christ. (1:5-8)*

This portion of Scripture proposes that faith comes before virtue, knowledge, temperance, patience, godliness, kindness and charity. Like faith, one can add that humility also precedes the other fruit since it was just established that both faith and humility are intertwined.

The final thought of this section comes from possibly the most used Scripture on works/rewards. This passage has been frequently misinterpreted by those promoting "Works Salvation." Its correct interpretation is that Godly works come only after repentance, faith and submission to Jesus Christ. James writes,

> *"Yea, a man may say, Thou hast faith, and I have works: shew me thy faith without thy works, and I will shew thee my faith by my works. Thou believest that there is one God; thou doest well: the devils also believe, and tremble. But wilt thou know, O vain man, that faith without works is dead?" (2:18-20)*

CHAPTER 14

MODELS OF HUMILITY

Examples

Now that the evidences, blessings and spiritual fruit of humility have been examined, it would be appropriate to bring them all together with a series of examples.

Moses

The first example of humility is found in the man who was the meekest man on earth: Moses (Num. 12:3). Amazingly, he was the meekest man on earth while yet being mighty in words and deeds (Acts 7:22). Moses left Egypt after killing an Egyptian that acted unjustly against a Hebrew.

> *By faith Moses, when he was come to years, refused to be called the son of Pharaoh's daughter; Choosing rather to suffer affliction with the people of God, than to enjoy the pleasures of sin for a season. (Heb. 11:24-25).*

This declaration indicates that Moses may have been able to stay in Egypt and face Pharaoh but it was God's plan for him to leave. His lowliness of heart also made him reject titles and seasonal pleasure instead choosing suffering with God's people.

Moreover, Moses thought nothing of himself (Exod. 3:11), cried unto the Lord in prayer (Exod. 15:25), did everything that the Lord commanded him to do (Exod. 40:16), fell upon his face (Num. 16:4), gave God the credit for miraculous works (Num. 16:28), felt that he was not eloquent/quick-tongued (Exod. 4:10) and had uncircumcised lips (Exod. 6:30). It is interesting that it is seldom preached that Moses lived one hundred twenty years (Deut. 34:7) that were equally divided into three distinct periods of humility. Moses' first period of life was marked by being a prince of Egypt, but yet he humbly chose his lineage over wealth and power. His second period of life was punctuated by him humbly raising a family (Exod. 2:21-22; 18:1-27) and being a shepherd (Exod. 3:1). His last forty-year period was marked by leading the Israelites out of Egypt and humbly guiding them through the wilderness. (Deut. 8:2; Josh. 5:6; Acts 7:36). God mightily blessed Moses' meekness by having the Bible's longest two-way divine dialog where many miraculous wonders were achieved (Deut. 8:2; Josh. 5:6; Acts 7:36).

Abraham

Before Moses, the example of humility came from Abraham, the Patriarch. Abraham, like the great majority of Bible characters, was presented in Scripture as a complex man. The accounts of him twice offering half-truths about his wife Sarah illustrate this fact. Nevertheless, Abraham was truly a humble servant of God who also displayed his humbleness toward fellow man. The Bible shows how Abram humbly took the land that his nephew Lot did not want in order to avoid strife. Genesis 13:9 proclaims,

> *"Is not the whole land before thee? separate thyself, I pray thee, from me: if thou wilt take the left hand, then I will go to the right; or if thou depart to the right hand, then I will go to the left."*

At this point God had not yet changed his name, but at age ninety-nine, Abram received his new name, Abraham, along with an "everlasting covenant" that had him "Fathering" many nations, and his circumcised descendants forever possessing the "Promised Land." (Gen. 17:1-14). One also reads in Genesis chapter 18 of Abraham deferentially but effectively interceding for the lives of Sodom's inhabitants with the pre-incarnate Jesus Christ. As he entreated with the Lord, he recognized his utter lowness in comparison to God.

> *And Abraham answered and said, Behold now, I have taken upon me to speak unto the Lord, which am but dust and ashes. (Gen. 18:27)*

As previously mentioned, Abraham also meekly bowed in the presence of the Lord (18:2) and in the presence of esteemed brethren (23:7-12).

Joseph

The next illustration of humility comes from Jacob's eleventh son, Joseph. While books can be written about Joseph's life and humility, this study will attempt only to address the most salient aspects of his earthly existence. It is first noticed that young Joseph displays humility and reverence toward his father through complete obedience. This is demonstrated by his feeding of the flocks and bringing home "intelligence" on the family business (Gen. 37:2, 13). Following his dreams and the jealousy of his brothers, Joseph is stripped of his coat, thrown into a pit, and sold twice as a slave, eventually landing at Potiphar's house in Egypt. Rewarded by God with the title of "House Overseer," Joseph is falsely accused because of his chasteness and is again abased as he is thrown back into prison. The Scriptures never suggest that Joseph complained or murmured but rather showcase his patience, integrity and concern for others. Once again, God blesses him:

> But the LORD was with Joseph, and shewed him mercy, and gave him favour in the sight of the keeper of the prison. (39:21)

The familiar record states that Joseph was ultimately released from prison due to accurately interpreting three dreams, the last of which was Pharaoh's. Through this last interpretation, at the age of thirty, God exalts Joseph to "second-in-command" behind Pharaoh. Joseph remains humble even though he is prospered and given preeminence.

Several years later, one reads of Joseph's interaction with his family. And while some would rightly conclude that he behaved duplicitously, overall he exhibited restraint and concern, especially for his father and younger brother. Quite possibly the most astounding aspect of Joseph's humility is how often he cried. The Scriptures inform us that he wept on six distinct occasions. (Gen. 42:24; 43:30; 45:2; 14-15; 46:29; 50:17). This proves that men who are powerful, successful, and love God, can weep; and weep often. Finally, Biblicists know that it was God's plan all along to create envy and evil in the early life of Joseph in order to bring him to and exalt him in Egypt. Once there, he would bring all of his kindred, keeping them separate from other nations and prospering them physically and numerically. This certainly would not have happened had they stayed in Canaan. Even Joseph knew that God meant for all that wickedness to be intended for good (Gen. 50:20)!

Job

No review of Biblical humility would be complete without mentioning the man who may have suffered more than anyone else; Job. One immediately reads that Job was a model of humility as he was described by the Bible as "perfect and upright, and one that feared God, and eschewed evil." (Job 1:1) Even after he lost all of his animals, all of his servants (except one) and all of his ten children, Job continued to display humility. He rent his mantle, shaved his head, fell to ground in worship and recited,

> *"...Naked came I out of my mother's womb, and naked shall I return thither: the LORD gave, and the LORD hath taken away; blessed be the name of the LORD. In all this Job sinned not, nor charged God foolishly." (Job. 1:21-22)*

His humility continued as boils covered his body and as his wife asked him to curse a Holy God. Regarding his wife's inappropriate comment, Job responds,

> *"Thou speakest as one of the foolish women speaketh. What? shall we receive good at the hand of God, and shall we not receive evil? In all this did not Job sin with his lips." (Job 2:10)*

Job rightly understood that one should receive evil as well as good. Both events should draw persons nigh to God. This is what James referred to when he wrote of "the patience of Job." (Jas. 5:11) It should be noted that in chapter three, Job questions his very life and existence but never curses Almighty God. After lengthy conversations with three well-intended, but misguided, visitor friends, Job was adamant that he was "righteous in his own eyes" (32:1) and that his calamity was not brought on by any active sin in his life. (*As examined earlier in the study, humility is also having an accurate and sober assessment of oneself as described in Romans 12:3; otherwise it becomes false humility and hence, pride.*) After the fourth visitor spoke (self-righteous Elihu), it became God's turn to speak to Job. Beginning with, "Where wast thou when I laid the foundations of the earth? declare, if thou hast understanding." (38:4) and ending with questions about the massive Leviathan (Sea Dinosaur), the Almighty proceeds to give Job a series of rhetorical questions that summarily convict Job of his smallness compared to God. It also purges him of any self-pity (again pride). Job ultimately responds to God's questions with a final humble declaration:

> *I know that thou canst do every thing, and that no thought can be withholden from thee. Who is he that hideth counsel without knowledge? therefore have I uttered that I understood not; things too wonderful for me, which I knew not. Hear, I beseech thee, and I will speak: I will demand of thee, and declare thou unto me. I have heard of thee by the hearing of the ear: but now mine eye seeth thee. Wherefore I abhor myself, and repent in dust and ashes. (Job. 42:2-6)*

After this lowly statement, God righteously rewards Job by blessing him with ten more children and likewise doubly restoring all his other earthly possessions. Not surprisingly, God also gives him long life to one hundred forty years of age.

Hannah

Next is a revisited example of abasement that not only impacted the future monarchy of Israel but also influenced the earthly life of the eternal Monarch, Jesus Christ. Hannah, Samuel's mother, can be rightly considered as one of the most humble women of the Bible. After being belittled by her husband's other wife for barrenness, Hannah made a most sincere and humble vow:

> *O LORD of hosts, if thou wilt indeed look on the affliction of thine handmaid, and remember me, and not forget thine handmaid, but wilt give unto thine handmaid a man child, then I will give him unto the LORD all the days of his life, and there shall no razor come upon his head. (1 Sam. 1:11)*

Accused of drunkenness by the prophet Eli during this prayer, she rightly answers that she was not a "daughter of Belial" but rather had completely submitted her soul to God. Once conceiving and birthing Samuel, Hannah makes a bullock sacrifice and honors her self-effacing vow by bringing her son to the prophet for training, after which she recites one of the most lovely praises and prophecies to be found in Scripture:

> *And Hannah prayed, and said, My heart rejoiceth in the LORD, mine horn is exalted in the LORD: my mouth is enlarged over mine enemies; because I rejoice in thy salvation. There is none holy as the LORD: for there is none beside thee: neither is there any rock like our God. Talk no more so exceeding proudly; let not arrogancy come out of your mouth: for the LORD is a God of knowledge, and by him actions are weighed. The bows of the mighty men are broken, and they that stumbled are girded with strength. They that were full have hired out themselves for bread; and they that were hungry ceased: so that the barren hath born seven; and she that hath many children is waxed feeble. The LORD killeth, and maketh alive: he bringeth down to the grave, and bringeth up. The LORD maketh poor, and maketh rich: he bringeth low, and lifteth up. He raiseth up the poor out of the dust, and lifteth up the beggar from the dunghill, to set them among princes, and to make them inherit the throne of glory: for the pillars of the earth are the LORD'S, and he hath set the world upon them. He will keep the feet of his saints, and the wicked shall be silent in darkness; for by strength shall no man prevail. The adversaries of the LORD shall be broken to pieces; out of heaven shall he thunder upon them: the LORD shall*

judge the ends of the earth; and he shall give strength unto his king, and exalt the horn of his anointed. (1 Sam. 2:1-10)

Hannah's legacy is noteworthy. Her son Samuel eventually anoints the first two kings of Israel and becomes the only man in the Holy Canon to have held all three titles of Judge, Prophet and Nazarite. Most notable is that several portions of her "Song of Thankfulness" were reiterated by Mary for her similar praise and prayer, called by scholars "The Song of Praise (Luke 1:46-55). (This blessed oratory will be explored shortly.)

Isaiah

The subsequent example, the prophet Isaiah, was a contemporary of the Southern Kings, Uzziah, Jotham, Ahaz and Hezekiah. Some even say that he lived until the reign of evil King, Manasseh. While Isaiah witnessed the Assyrian captivity of the Northern Kingdom, his primary emphasis was Judah. His most distinguished humble deed was walking naked and barefoot three years as a sign and wonder upon Egypt and upon Ethiopia (Isa. 20:3). Isaiah also made several humble proclamations. First, he admitted his unworthiness to the seraphim: *"Woe is me! for I am undone; because I am a man of unclean lips, and I dwell in the midst of a people of unclean lips: for mine eyes have seen the King, the LORD of hosts"* (6:5). While speaking of the Assyrian army being used by God as an instrument to humble Samaria, he sets a metaphorical precedent of man being a simple instrument in the hands of the Almighty: *"Shall the axe boast itself against him that heweth therewith? or shall the saw magnify itself against him that shaketh it? as if the rod should shake itself against them that lift it up, or as if the staff should lift up itself, as if it were no wood"* (Isa. 10:15). This metaphorical style was also used by Jeremiah and slightly altered later by Paul of Tarsus (Jer. 51:20-23; Rom. 9:20-21). Isaiah also famously declared to King Hezekiah, *"Thus saith the LORD, Set thine house in order: for thou shalt die, and not live"* (38:1). In summary, Isaiah was truly a humble servant of God whose zeal was overmatched only by his faith.

King Josiah

Returning to Judah's Davidic line of rulers, the marvelous narrative of King Josiah's humility is one that has inspired millions for over 2,600 years. Like some people of today, Josiah's lineage was not a Godly one. God's Words state that his father, Amon, and his grandfather, Manasseh, were abominable kings; the worst that Judah had known to date. In Second Kings chapter 21, God largely proclaimed judgment on Judah and Jerusalem because of their idolatry, evil abominations, and shedding of much innocent blood sanctioned by King Manasseh. His son, Amon, conspired just as wickedly. In fact, he was so evil that his personal servants killed him in his very own house. So what exactly did Josiah inherit in the first eight years of his life? A kingdom and a most dysfunctional and foul upbringing. Even with that background, one straightaway reads of Josiah's humility before God.

And he did that which was right in the sight of the LORD, and walked in all the way of David his father, and turned not aside to the right hand or to the left. (2 Kgs. 22:2)

One also finds that at the still young age of twenty-six (eighteenth year of his reign), an "old" book of the law was "found" and read aloud to Josiah. It apparently was a part of the law that had not been read for some period of time; perhaps having been hidden or discarded by Manasseh or Amon. A Christian must not forget that God has promised to preserve every single one of His precious Words. They are extant.

The words of the LORD are pure words: as silver tried in a furnace of earth, purified seven times. Thou shalt keep them, O LORD, thou shalt preserve them from this generation for ever. (Psa. 12:6-7)

Upon hearing the previously discarded book, Josiah "rent his clothes" and began to inquire about the sentence that had been imposed on his fathers. Josiah was rightly concerned about the Lord's impending wrath. This is how God responded:

> *Because thine heart was tender, and thou hast humbled thyself before the LORD, when thou heardest what I spake against this place, and against the inhabitants thereof, that they should become a desolation and a curse, and hast rent thy clothes, and wept before me; I also have heard thee, saith the LORD. (2 Kgs. 22:19)*

Josiah justly continues his humility before God by making a covenant to:

> *...walk after the LORD, and to keep his commandments and his testimonies and his statutes with all their heart and all their soul, to perform the words of this covenant that were written in this book. (2 Kgs. 23:3)*

Amazingly, all of Judah likewise made this covenant. *Josiah then demonstrates the zeal that all Christians should possess as he quickly and methodically starts purging Judah of evil by destroying demonic objects (Baal images, altars, groves, houses of sodomy and high places of occultic worship built by Solomon), eliminating demonic practices (fires to Molech, burning incense in Temple, moving of bones and worshipping celestial bodies), and punishing or killing ones that had handed over their lives to Satan (idolatrous priests, wizards and workers of familiar spirits) (2 Kgs. 23).* There was no compromise with any form of evil with Josiah. Regrettably, this is something that is missing even in the most fundamental of churches as too many are concerned with *offending*. Thus, people erroneously "bite their lips" when others watch grossly inappropriate movies, speak glowingly of "questionable" people and practices, listen to clearly unacceptable music, dress in sexually immodest ways, and move in provocative manner, for fear of alienating. Josiah would not have had a single compunction for this type of exposing and eradicating. Lastly, Josiah was not just about eliminating the bad; he also knew how to put on a Godly party. After ridding Judah of evil and all appearances thereof, the Bible declares that Jerusalem celebrated Passover in a manner that had not been experienced since the "days of the judges that judged Israel." Plausibly, over four hundred fifty Passovers had elapsed since the Passover celebrations had been that good. All were present; the priests, Levites and all Judah and Israel (2 Kgs. 23:22; 2 Chr. 35:18). It verifies that true "fun" comes from living virtuous and upright lives.

Through the record of Josiah, the Bible also teaches that one can have wicked and prideful ancestors but still be transformed by the Spirit of God and His Words! It also is a message of individual and national hope.

> *And like unto him was there no king before him, that turned to the LORD with all his heart, and with all his soul, and with all his might, according to all the law of Moses; neither after him arose there any like him. (2 Kgs. 23:25)*

Daniel

Jumping forward just a generation or so, one encounters the only humble prophet (of the many found in Scriptures) that was exiled from his adolescent home, lived under three distinct kingdoms, served multiple rulers, experienced life-threatening persecution, and still delivered prophecies, some of which were fulfilled, and some which are still awaiting fulfillment. This of course is the prophet Daniel. In Daniel 1:4, Bible readers learn early on that Daniel was a perfect candidate for pride since he was healthy, handsome, wise, intelligent, and had excellent social skills. He was also an unparalleled dream interpreter, who was set by Babylonian King Darius over the presidents and princes (6:3). Even with "everything" going for him, he still demonstrated humility by not eating the defiled king's meat (1:8), answering gracefully during trials (2:15), blessing and giving God all the glory (2:20-23, 28; 6:22), defending others (2:24), remembering his companions during times of prosperity (2:49), not accepting gifts for his God-given talents (5:17), being found blameless among his enemies (6:5), and respectfully acknowledging other prophets (9:2). Nowhere to be found is a proud or accusatorial statement by Daniel, even after being treacherously thrown into the lion's den by the schemes of his envious contemporaries. On the contrary, his first comments from the den were humble and selfless: *"O king, live for ever"* (6:21). Of intrigue is Daniel's humble admission of not being able to understand several pivotal end-time prophecies which he saw and penned:

> *And I heard, but I understood not: then said I, O my Lord, what shall be the end of these things? (12:8)*

Possibly even more telling is that God actually meant for no one to understand his tribulation prophecies until latter times; likely these times (Daniel 12:9-10).

Joseph and Mary

Moving to the New Testament, the first examples of humility come from the earthly parents of the Redeemer Messiah; Joseph and Mary. Both of these choice servants demonstrated true humility and gentleness in the course of their betrothal and marriage periods. They even quietly marveled at the things spoken of their son. Mary, outliving Joseph, continued displaying meekness throughout Christ's adult ministry and death. First, she accepts her culturally humiliating out-of-wedlock pregnancy with humble submission. Mary simply says,

> *"Behold the handmaid of the Lord; be it unto me according to thy word. And the angel departed from her."*
> *(Luke 1:38)*

However, to really examine Mary's humility one must read the lovely discourse called by many "Mary's Song of Praise" or "Magnificat." This segment is called such because it rightly magnifies God to His proper station. So beautiful is this praise and prayer that it merits being shown in its entirety.

> *And Mary said, My soul doth magnify the Lord, And my spirit hath rejoiced in God my Saviour. For he hath regarded the low estate of his handmaiden: for, behold, from henceforth all generations shall call me blessed. For he that is mighty hath done to me great things; and holy is his name. And his mercy is on them that fear him*

from generation to generation. He hath shewed strength with his arm; he hath scattered the proud in the imagination of their hearts. He hath put down the mighty from their seats, and exalted them of low degree. He hath filled the hungry with good things; and the rich he hath sent empty away. He hath holpen his servant Israel, in remembrance of his mercy; As he spake to our fathers, to Abraham, and to his seed for ever. (Luke 1:46-55)

There are also several examples of Mary's humility throughout Christ's adult ministry. One first witnesses Mary's rightful submission to her Son at the Cana wedding:

His mother saith unto the servants, Whatsoever he saith unto you, do it. (John. 2:5)

One then reads of Mary supporting Christ's ministry in different towns (Mark 3:31; Luke 8:19; John 2:12), being at the foot of the cross, (Matt. 12:47; Mark 15:40; John 19: 25), and submitting to being taken care of by John the Apostle (Jn. 19:26-27). After her Son's ascension, Mary is found in communion with the Apostles and other disciples:

These all continued with one accord in prayer and supplication, with the women, and Mary the mother of Jesus, and with his brethren. (Acts. 1:14)

Although not directly confirmed in God's Words, it is very likely that Mary was also present during the appearance of the Holy Spirit at Pentecost as the Bible almost identically testifies *"they were all with one accord in one place"* (Acts 2:1). Appropriately, the earthly mother of God was present at the commencement of the church age.

Turning solely to Joseph (son of Jacob), the Bible called him a just man as manifested by his unwillingness to make a public example of Mary's unexpected pregnancy and his preference to put her away privily (Matt. 1:19). He obviously did not feel the need to have his "proud" manhood vindicated. After witnessing a divine revelation that Mary had conceived of the Holy Ghost and was carrying the Messiah, Joseph humbly refrained from his legal right of intimately "knowing" Mary, until her firstborn, Jesus, was born (Matt. 1:25). (Explicit in this statement is that Mary was not a virgin throughout her whole life and that she had more children both of which are flagrant omissions in Roman Catholic teachings.) Lastly, one reads of Joseph humbly and immediately obeying no less than three angelic commands (1:24; 2:13-14, 20-21) that both preserved his family and fulfilled Old Testament prophecy.

John the Baptist

The next model of humility comes from Christ's very cousin, John the Baptist or the Immerser, (so-called because the word "baptize" means "total immersion"). Born of meek servants of God (Zacharias the priest and Elisabeth), John preached the baptism of repentance for the remission of sins (Mark 1:4) and prepared the way of the Lord (Luke 3:4). The Bible provides several humble acknowledgements of John's unworthiness compared to the coming Messiah. First, before knowing who the Messiah would be, John humbly declared,

> *"I indeed baptize you with water unto repentance: but he that cometh after me is mightier than I, whose shoes I am not worthy to bear: he shall baptize you with the Holy Ghost, and with fire." (Matt. 3:11)*

Second, upon seeing Jesus at the Jordan while baptizing, John said,

> *"...I have need to be baptized of thee, and comest thou to me?" (Matt. 3:14)*

Lastly, having realized that the significant part of his ministry had concluded, John recognized the need to yield to a greater and more important ministry:

> *John answered and said, A man can receive nothing, except it be given him from heaven. Ye yourselves bear me witness, that I said, I am not the Christ, but that I am sent before him. He that hath the bride is the bridegroom: but the friend of the bridegroom, which standeth and heareth him, rejoiceth greatly because of the bridegroom's voice: this my joy therefore is fulfilled. He must increase, but I must decrease. (John. 3:27-30)*

The Scriptures also inform us that John ate and dressed modestly (Matt. 3:4), did not drink wine or strong drink (Luke 1:15), would often fast and pray with his disciples (Matt. 9:14; Luke 5:33), scolded the sins of Herod (Matt. 14:4; Mark 6:18; Luke 3:19), admonished the sins of Israel (Luke 3:7), and did works in the spirit of Elijah (Matt. 17:12-13; Luke 1:17). Most importantly, one reads that he was indwelt with the Holy Ghost upon being conceived (Luke 1:15). All of these works would have been impossible otherwise. Even the Lord Jesus Christ attested to John's humbleness when he declared,

> *"Verily I say unto you, Among them that are born of women there hath not risen a greater than John the Baptist: notwithstanding he that is least in the kingdom of heaven is greater than he." (Matt. 11:11)*

As great as John the Immerser was, our Savior interestingly lets brethren of all ages know how they can be greater than he; Christ simply tells them just to be the least in the kingdom of heaven.

Paul

The final Biblical example of humility comes from Paul of Tarsus (formerly Saul). Luke's writings concerning Paul in the book of Acts affirm Paul's humility:

> *And when they were come to him, he said unto them, Ye know, from the first day that I came into Asia, after what manner I have been with you at all seasons, serving the LORD with all humility of mind, and with many tears, and temptations, which befell me by the lying in wait of the Jews." (Acts 20:18-19)*

Paul also writes in his first epistle to the church at Corinth:

> *And lest I should be exalted above measure through the abundance of the revelations, there was given to me a thorn in the flesh, the messenger of Satan to buffet me, lest I should be exalted above measure. For this thing I besought the Lord thrice, that it might depart from me. And he said unto me, My grace is sufficient for thee: for my strength is made perfect in weakness. Most gladly*

therefore will I rather glory in my infirmities, that the power of Christ may rest upon me. Therefore I take pleasure in infirmities, in reproaches, in necessities, in persecutions, in distresses for Christ's sake: for when I am weak, then am I strong. (2 Cor. 12:7-10)

Paul not only accepted his trials and weaknesses but thought them necessary. For he understood that true strength only comes from Lord Jesus, especially when one is abased and suffering need (Phil. 4:12).

Paul also gave himself up to ministry through long hours of preaching (Acts 20:9) and tarrying (1 Cor. 16:8; 1 Tim. 3:15). More importantly, he understood that ministry is only possible if God permits it to occur (Rom. 9:22; 1 Cor. 16:7; Heb. 6:3). Paul was able to live this way because he thought lowly of himself. He viewed himself as the chief of all sinners (1 Tim. 1:15), the least of the apostles (1 Cor. 15:9), and that in his flesh dwelleth no good thing (Rom. 7:18). As such, he would present himself base and lowly in person (2 Cor. 10:1) and was reticent to boast, even though he was one of the few chosen apostles (2 Cor. 10:8). No doubt, these were not the Christian platitudes of today but rather sincere expressions of his past and his Adamic nature. Likewise, Paul cautioned believers to be wary of those that glory in their mere appearance (2 Cor. 5:12). *It should also be noted that while Paul was meek and humble he always expressed firmness in his doctrines and rebukes (1 Cor. 4:21).*

Not long before being martyred for his faith and testimony in our Lord Jesus Christ, Paul offered these last humble words to encourage those who may be suffering from persecutions and to prepare others who soon may suffer a similar fate:

For I am now ready to be offered, and the time of my departure is at hand. I have fought a good fight, I have finished my course, I have kept the faith: Henceforth there is laid up for me a crown of righteousness, which the Lord, the righteous judge, shall give me at that day:

and not to me only, but unto all them also that love his appearing. (2 Tim. 4:6-8)

A believer's prayer should be to become as gracious and courageous as Paul was until his martyred end.

Humble Saints Not in the Bible

Outside of Scripture, there have been many saints that have lived self-effacing lives toward God and man. Early church fathers like Papias, Justin Martyr, Tertullian, Irenaeus and Clement of Alexandria were humble servants, many of whom were martyred. Later on, men like Michael Sattler, William Tyndale, John Bunyan, Roger Williams, John Clarke, William Carey, Richard Fuller, Thomas Baldwin, Adoniram Judson, Luther Rice, James Boyce, Dean Burgon, and D.L. Moody were Godly models of humility. The twentieth century has also produced humble servants like Eric Liddell, Harry Ironside, Clarence Larkin, Philip Mauro, J. Vernon McGee, John R. Rice, Charles Ryrie and thousands of other men and women who work tirelessly for the Lord but may never receive glory from man; only heavenly crowns.

Remaining in the twenty-first century and returning to athletics, football coach Tony Dungy offers a contemporary example of humility. Mr. Dungy, a publically professing Christian, cited former Dallas Cowboy Hall of Fame coach, Tom Landry, as being an example of humility in an era marked by increasing egotism. In his book, *Uncommon,* Mr. Dungy said of Mr. Landry,

"He was a quiet man. At times he seemed almost shy, but it was simply his humility before God and man."[68]

"Tom Landry's life was not about him; it was one of submission to the God he followed."[69]

Those who watched football from the 1960's through the 1980's can recall coach Landry's temperance during Super Bowl victories as well as in times of defeat. Likewise,

---

[68] Tony Dungy, <u>Uncommon</u> (Carol Stream, IL: Tyndale House, 2009), 24.
[69] Ibid., 25.

Coach Dungy has showcased humility in his many wins and difficult defeats on the football field as well as in his personal life as observed after the suicide of his eldest son. Other notable athletes that have professed Christ and have outwardly and consistently manifested humility are: A.C. Green, Curt Warner, Mariano Rivera, Albert Pujols and Tim Tebow.

A Special Case of Humility: Jason Wright

A truly unique illustration of humility comes from a non-famous NFL player who left the league to pursue a life serving Jesus Christ. Jason Wright, who spent seven seasons in the NFL, retired from being an Arizona Cardinal Special Teams Captain and his $1 million per year salary in September 2011. The reason why he left? Mr. Wright provides an answer. "What's the motive behind me playing longer? What is it in there that draws me? So people would know my name? For me, it was superficial. For me and my family, and our belief in God, it wasn't a good enough motivation."[70] Only twenty-nine years old, he appears not to be driven by self-glory or financial remuneration but by a desire to follow God's will. Even his teammates acknowledge his Godly intentions. Five-time Pro Bowl Wide-Receiver, Larry Fitzgerald says,

> "He's one of the best teammates I've ever had. But Jason has a higher calling, and he goes by the Lord's plan. As a friend and a Christian, I admire his courage."[71]

The loving husband and father of three children (one of whom is adopted), is planning to earn his MBA. After finishing his schooling, he meekly admits not quite knowing what his future holds, but hints that he may work with disadvantaged youth (which is how he and his wife adopted a then teenage girl). Regarding the accolades and successes he has received over the years, Mr. Wright humbly declares,

---

[70] Sean Jensen, "Jason Wright passes up NFL contract to attend business school". Yahoo! Sports. September 20, 2011.
[71] Ibid.

"I just say glory to God. There's no doubt he's working through us, because we're not that great."[72] Praise God that there are still selfless stories of people leaving careers, fame, and fortune to serve the Lord. Believers should pray that God may use Mr. Wright's previous professional experience to reach the unsaved and be an example to "silent" Christians through his devotion to God.

A Special Case of Humility: Danny and Tracy Kofke

The last example of humility comes from a lovely family that lives unpretentiously and deferentially. Danny and Tracy Kofke have been showing thousands of families how a family of four can survive on an income of $40,000 per year. They have written two books on stewardship called, *How to Survive (and Perhaps Thrive) on a Teacher's Salary* and *A Simple Book of Financial Wisdom*. In these books, they have basically shown others how they humbly live on one salary, have mom nurturing the children at home, and purchase only what they really need. Included in their approach is the critical aspect of training their children to think and behave in like manner. At the core, their attitude is about living to please God and purging themselves of the covetousness that comes from sinful pride. Mr. Kofke states:

> Pride is sometimes a hard thing to swallow, but I knew that many of these people were not making smart financial decisions and these decisions would eventually come back and hurt them. I don't know if it is unusual advice but, when making financial decisions, you have to do what is right for you and not be influenced by the many temptations that surround us.[73]

How often have western Christians mimicked the consumerism of the world only to be, at best, distracted from the things of God, or, at worst, to be enslaved by payments and dual working situations? Because of "not

---

[72] Ibid.

[73] Kimberly Palmer, " The Secret to Living Well on $40,000 a Year". U.S. News and World Report. September 23, 2011.

making smart decisions" and confusing wants with needs, many will deceive themselves into thinking that a family cannot accomplish what the Kofke's are achieving, even with double or triple the income. Believers should recognize pride for what it is; a Satanic snare.

Besides the basic tenets of faith in Christ, prayer, and Scripture reading, the Kofke's are honest about the difficulties inherent in living this way in a world filled with avarice.

> "Living below my means is the toughest rule for me to follow. There are so many temptations — Madison Avenue spends billions of dollars each year to get our money — and sometimes I want to buy things I know I should not."[74]

Part of the solution comes from understanding the spiritual aspect, which invariably impacts the emotional aspect. Praise God for giving this dear family the clarity of heart and mind to make decisions for the Lord and to be a light for millions that are struggling, even as they earn far greater incomes.

---

[74] Ibid.

CHAPTER 15

BOTH SIDES OF THE FENCE

The Bible's Accurate Depiction of Man

Those who unadvisedly say that the Bible has been "cleansed" to only portray positive things about characters and events, have apparently not read through the world's only Holy Book. If they had read solely through one or two books, they would have been exposed to the many human frailties and oft inconsistencies among God's patriarchs, judges, priests, kings, prophets and apostles. God's Words depict Godly people committing sin and portray evil people repenting and living to please God. These records were given to us by the inspiration of the Holy Spirit. Why? The answers are straightforward; God desired man to know that all are fallen sinners and that He can work His miraculous wonders through imperfect vessels (such as all believers) to accomplish His Holy will.

Examples of Humility and Pride

With that as commentary, it is time to examine several Scriptural characters who have exemplified both humility and pride over the course of their lives.

King David

David's Humility

The first example comes from the youngest son of Jesse; King David. Many volumes have been written about his relationship with God, with others, and his many feats of heroism. This analysis will only attempt to present a quick survey of his life. Regarding his humble roots, the Bible discloses that he was a lowly shepherd boy (1 Sam. 16:11) who submitted to his father's authority (17:15, 20) and knew his station in life (18:23). Scripture depicts his fearless stance and humble reliance on God against Goliath and the Philistines (17:45-47). The Bible also describes how David continued to meekly serve Saul for many years after learning that he would be his successor (16:23; 17:58; 18:5; 24:8-15). David would humbly call Saul "father" or "my lord." One also reads that David was not too proud to rejoice in dance to celebrate the entry of the "Ark of the Lord" into Jerusalem (2 Sam. 6:16). Lastly, it is interesting to note that David commonly grieved openly when tragedy or unrighteousness ensued. (1 Sam. 30:4; 2 Sam. 1:11-12; 12:22; 13:31; Psa. 69:10). As affirmed earlier, proud people have difficulty crying publicly or even privately; especially men.

When examining David's humility, one must consider his many extant psalms on meekness and lowliness of heart. These psalms have provided comfort and solace to hundreds of millions of believers over the centuries. Some of his better known psalms on meekness and humility are:

When he maketh inquisition for blood, he remembereth them: he forgetteth not the cry of the humble." (Ps. 9:12)

LORD, thou hast heard the desire of the humble: thou wilt prepare their heart, thou wilt cause thine ear to hear." (Ps. 10:17)

But I am a worm, and no man; a reproach of men, and despised of the people. (Ps. 22:6)

"The meek will he guide in judgment: and the meek will he teach his way." (Ps. 25:9)

My soul shall make her boast in the LORD: the humble shall hear thereof, and be glad. (Ps. 34:2)

The humble shall see this, and be glad: and your heart shall live that seek God. (Ps. 69:32)

One must also acknowledge that David humbly foreknew that his kingly descendant (Lord Jesus Christ) would rule forever at the right hand of the Father.

For David himself said by the Holy Ghost, The LORD said to my Lord, Sit thou on my right hand, till I make thine enemies thy footstool. David therefore himself calleth him Lord; and whence is he then his son? And the common people heard him gladly. (Mark. 12:36-37)

David was effectively saying that he was son of his Son!

Finally, a mention of David's exhortation to his son is appropriate. In humble fashion, David keeps God first in his ending charge to soon-to-be-king Solomon:

> *I go the way of all the earth: be thou strong therefore, and shew thyself a man; And keep the charge of the LORD thy God, to walk in his ways, to keep his statutes, and his commandments, and his judgments, and his testimonies, as it is written in the law of Moses, that thou mayest prosper in all that thou doest, and whithersoever thou turnest thyself: That the LORD may continue his word which he spake concerning me, saying, If thy children take heed to their way, to walk before me in truth with all their heart and with all their soul, there shall not fail thee (said he) a man on the throne of Israel. (1 Kgs. 2:2-4)*

David's Pride

While Scriptures disclose that David was a man after God's heart (1 Sam. 13:14; Acts 13:22), it also spectacularly shows that he was not a perfect man. Pride of the heart manifested itself in at least two different occasions. This seeming contradiction has posed problems for students of the Canon of Scripture as well as lent ammunition for those who are at enmity with God. A full response to the question of how a man after God's heart can sin and affect so many people will not be attempted in this analysis. Suffice to say that God's ways are unsearchable. More tangibly, one must restate that all men are sinners; even life-long, mature Christians. Confirming this eternal truth, John the beloved wrote,

> *"If we say that we have not sinned, we make him a liar, and his word is not in us." (1 John. 1:10)*

David's initial display of pride is the most known, even among unbelievers. In this chronicle, one reads of David's lustful desire to have the wife (Bathsheba) of one of his loyal soldiers (Uriah). His evil schemes lure the married woman into committing adultery, resulting in an immediate conception. This unforeseen pregnancy forces David to plot further. He asks General Joab to bring Uriah back from the battle lines with the hope of creating a romantic marriage interlude (between Uriah and Bathsheba) that would be close enough to the conception date to avoid scrutiny. The king then eats, speaks, and conveys hospitality to the soldier, to either gain his confidence or to perhaps ease some guilt. When Uriah refuses to leave David's side because of his loyalty to the king, David conspires with Joab to have Uriah moved to a combat zone that guaranteed sure death (2 Sam. 11). Once Uriah met with his death, David continued with his haughtiness through his self-righteous attitude. The prophet Nathan cleverly exposed the king's hypocrisy through David's strong condemnation of someone else's sin while not even recognizing his own comparable sin (2 Sam. 12:1-13). Are not people similar today? They are concerned with the mote in someone else's eye but ignore the beam in their own. In effect, *man's pride blinds him of his own sin and makes him focus on the sins of others*. Aside from the deep shame felt by the king, Nathan next decrees a series of consequences that will plague David for the rest of his life:

> *Howbeit, because by this deed thou hast given great occasion to the enemies of the LORD to blaspheme, the child also that is born unto thee shall surely die. (2 Sam. 12:14)*

This grave error and subsequent tragedy were used by God to fill David with a repentant heart, enabling him to write many of his lowly Psalms. Just imagine a Bible without Psalm 51. This precious Psalm attests that God humbles and shames the proud. The first six verses of this convicting Psalm are:

> *To the chief Musician, A Psalm of David, when Nathan the prophet came unto him, after he had gone in to Bathsheba. Have mercy upon me, O God, according to thy lovingkindness: according unto the multitude of thy tender mercies blot out my transgressions. Wash me throughly from mine iniquity, and cleanse me from my sin. For I acknowledge my transgressions: and my sin is*

ever before me. Against thee, thee only, have I sinned, and done this evil in thy sight: that thou mightest be justified when thou speakest, and be clear when thou judgest. Behold, I was shapen in iniquity; and in sin did my mother conceive me. Behold, thou desirest truth in the inward parts: and in the hidden part thou shalt make me to know wisdom.

David's second act of pride is far lesser known but actually worse in God's eyes since it was called a "great sin." In Second Samuel chapter 24, the Bible depicts how David delighted in numbering all of his subjects and mighty warriors throughout Israel and Judah. David wanted to know his strength and the strength of his armies. He was essentially trusting in worldly assets and not in the Lord. It is akin to counting and delighting in the monetary value of a 401k or a home's assessed selling value. One should never forget the Lord's Words on this very matter:

And the disciples were astonished at his words. But Jesus answereth again, and saith unto them, Children, how hard is it for them that trust in riches to enter into the kingdom of God! (Mark 10:24)

The major consequence of David's second act of arrogance was severe, as 70,000 Israelites perished in a three-day pestilence (2 Sam. 24:15).

Returning to the account of the famous battle with Goliath and the Philistines, it is curious to note that David's brothers thought that his courage was a result of pride and "naughtiness of heart" (17:28). (Could it have been that David previously displayed prideful behaviors? If so, it could be a clue as to what would happen later in his life.) David's response to his brothers was equally peculiar as he almost sounded like someone who was always getting into mischief by stating,

"...What have I now done? Is there not a cause?" (17:29)

Quite possibly the greatest difference between David and many other prideful sinners was his heart condition. The

Scriptures show how David's heart would truly regret and repent. It was not just a public exhibition to gain empathy but a state of lowliness that engulfed him. He mourned death, sin and estrangement. David's heart may have been one of the reasons he was chosen by God to enter into an everlasting Covenant whereby his seed would eternally reign through the Messiah. This covenant is unilateral, as validated by the fact that many of David's descendants did not walk with the Lord!

Solomon

The oldest surviving son of David and Bathsheba was none other than King Solomon. His story is one of the more perplexing found in all mankind. Solomon was raised in David's house and was no doubt exposed to the singing of Psalms and the reading of God's Holy Words. He also experienced first-hand the consequences of sinful decisions; some of which were committed by his father. All this sets the stage for the moment he becomes king. Early in his reign, God appeared to Solomon in a night dream and offered to grant him what he wanted. Solomon's response was to humbly ask for governing wisdom, as he said, *"Give therefore thy servant an understanding heart to judge thy people, that I may discern between good and bad: for who is able to judge this thy so great a people"* (1 Kgs. 3:9)? This so pleased God that he not only gave him wisdom but also riches and honour. God conditionally decreed:

> *Behold, I have done according to thy words: lo, I have given thee a wise and an understanding heart; so that there was none like thee before thee, neither after thee shall any arise like unto thee. And I have also given thee that which thou hast not asked, both riches, and honour: so that there shall not be any among the kings like unto thee all thy days. And if thou wilt walk in my ways, to keep my statutes and my commandments, as thy father David did walk, then I will lengthen thy days. (1Kgs. 3:12-14)*

What more would a man need after this proclamation from the All-mighty? One reads that Solomon continued to humbly honor God by building the magnificent Temple and other structures, passing wise judgments, and by writing 3,000 proverbs and 1,005 songs (1 Kgs. 4:32). As such, God mightily blessed Solomon with riches, possessions, peace, power, and a forty-year reign.

The account of Solomon now begins to slowly turn as he proudly starts marrying women who do not worship the one true God, but rather worship satanic counterfeits. Intermarriage was easy for him since he had 700 wives and 300 concubines (1 Kgs. 11:3). These wives eventually turn Solomon's heart away from God. God said of these unequally yoked unions:

> But king Solomon loved many strange women, together with the daughter of Pharaoh, women of the Moabites, Ammonites, Edomites, Zidonians, and Hittites; Of the nations concerning which the LORD said unto the children of Israel, Ye shall not go in to them, neither shall they come in unto you: for surely they will turn away your heart after their gods: Solomon clave unto these in love. (1 Kgs. 11:1-2)

Solomon's prideful apostasy culminates in him building a "high-place" for his Egyptian wife so that she would not desecrate the Holy Temple. He then built similar structures for his other wives (Vs. 5-8). These pagan women then influenced others, including Solomon. So the flow was: 1) Marry pagan women; 2) Build them places of worship under "good" intentions of separation; 3) Eventually, many others (including Solomon) begin worshipping there. This becomes a tragic legacy for Solomon since these "high-places" stayed in Judah for over one hundred years until destroyed by King Jehoshaphat. (They likely stayed in the Northern Kingdom until the Assyrian captivity.)

Because of Solomon's haughty disobedience, several major consequences follow. God's Words declare:

> Notwithstanding in thy days I will not do it for David thy father's sake: but I will rend it out of the hand of thy son. Howbeit I will not rend away all the kingdom; but will give one tribe to thy son for David my servant's sake, and for

> *Jerusalem's sake which I have chosen. And the LORD stirred up an adversary unto Solomon, Hadad the Edomite: he was of the king's seed in Edom. (1 Kgs. 11:12-14)*

One also reads of his problems with Jeroboam (the eventual king of the Northern Tribes) and Shishak the King of Egypt. Because of God's conditional promise to Solomon, a thorough reading construes that his life was cut short at possibly around the age of sixty.

The chronicle takes a turn for the better as God is not finished using Solomon. A repentant and remorseful Solomon, late in life, scribes some of the most pointed warnings and lamentations found in Scripture. The book of Ecclesiastes is the humble narrative of a man who had it all and in greater quantities than anyone else that ever lived. What was Solomon's conclusion of having everything without God?

> *Vanity of vanities, saith the preacher; all is vanity. (Eccl. 12:8)*

Along those lines, one reads what were perhaps Solomon's final Biblical exhortations:

> *Let us hear the conclusion of the whole matter: Fear God, and keep his commandments: for this is the whole duty of man. For God shall bring every work into judgment, with every secret thing, whether it be good, or whether it be evil. (Eccl. 12:13-14)*

Finishing with true Godly wisdom, Solomon captures many of the great doctrines of the Old and New Testaments in just these two verses.

Rehoboam

Fittingly, the next example comes from Solomon's son and kingly successor, Rehoboam. He reigned from the age of forty-one for seventeen years. More than Solomon, Rehoboam was raised in an environment of political and financial security. He must have certainly been positively exposed to his father's proverbs, psalms and lamentations.

Likewise, he was also likely exposed to his father's ungodly marriage selections, gross excesses in marriage, and overall opulence. Therefore, it is not surprising that Rehoboam was able to demonstrate pride, and some small semblance of humility, during his lifetime.

It is relevant to begin the account of Rehoboam with a verse written to encapsulate his life.

> *And he did evil, because he prepared not his heart to seek the LORD. (2 Chr. 12:14)*

In essence, he was so full of self-direction that he did not seek God. Rehoboam thought that he could do it all himself. Scripture cites that he acted proudly by forsaking the counsel of wise old men and consulted with the young men that had grown up with him (1 Kgs. 12:8). He also crudely responds to the people's request of lowering the taxes by actually increasing their burden (1 Kgs. 12:13-14). Before moving further, believers should not be so quick in condemning Rehoboam, lest they think that not preparing the heart to seek the Lord is just reserved for Old Testament kings. Isn't it applicable to today's Christians? Aren't prayers half-hearted if done at all? Isn't it a challenge to spend fifteen minutes in His Words, but yet finding two hours to watch a sporting event, movie, check Facebook, play a video game, or cut the lawn doesn't present a problem? How often is congregating with likeminded believers to revere a Holy God simply a routine task, but a visit to a favorite restaurant, retail store, or amusement park is filled with dynamic enthusiasm? Why? In great part, the church has become the world! Christians have been seduced into believing that one can achieve all of God's promised power and not have to sacrifice a single thing that the world offers. Some incorrectly cite "liberty in Christ" only to become servants of corruption (2 Pet. 2:19). Numerous people judge others for working Sundays and not coming to church, but yet become part of the problem as they patronize businesses on Sunday incenting them to keep their doors open. Most people criticize society's appalling tailspin, but yet buy products from companies that are openly hostile to

God and His laws and who in turn support evil sinful practices. A good number ask themselves and others why they struggle with family, jobs, and finances. People wonder why there is fleeting joy and peace in their lives. Sadly, like Rehoboam, many have not prepared their hearts to seek the Lord. Unceasing prayer, reading Scripture, and worship, along with fellowship, are the foundations of preparing a heart to seek the Lord.

Coming back to Rehoboam, the Bible also reveals that evil proliferated in Judah during his early kingship:

> *And Judah did evil in the sight of the LORD, and they provoked him to jealousy with their sins which they had committed, above all that their fathers had done. For they also built them high places, and images, and groves, on every high hill, and under every green tree. And there were also sodomites in the land: and they did according to all the abominations of the nations which the LORD cast out before the children of Israel. (1 Kgs. 14:22-24)*

As long as Rehoboam was personally strengthened through wealth and kingdom stability, he arrogantly ignored the law of God (2 Chr. 12:1). Pride causes people to close their eyes to what is happening around them because they are only concerned about what directly impacts them. The selfish adages "as long as it does not affect me" and "all people are doing it" become mantras for anemic Christians who refuse to stand boldly for truth and righteousness.

In the midst of Rehoboam's sinful pride, he yet displayed some humility by obeying the prophet and not attacking Israel. Someone completely driven by ego would have disobediently attacked, either to consolidate power and/or to execute a punishment. The passage recites,

> *"Thus saith the LORD, Ye shall not go up, nor fight against your brethren: return every man to his house: for this thing is done of me. And they obeyed the words of the LORD, and returned from going against Jeroboam." (2 Chr. 11:4)*

As an interesting aside, Rehoboam may have quite possibly learned a humble lesson from his father's contemptible polygamy. God's Words state that he practiced relative moderation with women by "only" having eighteen wives and sixty concubines (2 Chr. 11:21). Thus, Rehoboam possessed only eight percent of the women that his father did. Most would not call this true humility but it was certainly a step in the right direction.

The review of Rehoboam concludes on a note of repentance. Like many, it took a dark set of circumstances to truly humble Rehoboam. As Egypt was about to conquer Judah, Shemaiah the prophet conveyed to Rehoboam and the princes the dire news of their unfaithfulness to God. The prophet declared,

> *"Thus saith the LORD, Ye have forsaken me, and therefore have I also left you in the hand of Shishak." (2 Chr. 12:5)*

After many years of ignoring the Lord in prosperity, Rehoboam and the princes had an immediate and appropriate response:

> *Whereupon the princes of Israel and the king humbled themselves; and they said, The LORD is righteous. (12:6)*

God seeing this lowly act of contrition gracefully spared Rehoboam and Judah from destruction and conquest (12:12), once again proving that God forgives a heart that repents!

King Jehoshaphat

An interesting example of "flip-flop" humility and pride is found with King Jehoshaphat of Judah. The great-great grandson of Solomon, he reigned from thirty-five years of age to sixty. A walking contradiction, Jehoshaphat was himself upright but did not initially purge wicked idolatry from Judah.

> *And he walked in all the ways of Asa his father; he turned not aside from it, doing that which was right in the*

> *eyes of the LORD: nevertheless the high places were*
> *not taken away; for the people offered and burnt incense*
> *yet in the high places. (1 Kgs. 22:43)*

This verse parallels some of today's liberal Christians who try to live their own lives for the Lord but refuse to be "salt" and "light" for others living in sin. The plain truth is that if a saint does not call sin what it is, then no one will! *Christians fool themselves if they believe that consequences for this sort of compromise will not be forthcoming.* In Jehoshaphat's case, the Scriptures declare that he later removed the "high" places and groves of Baal because the Lord lifted-up his heart. This change of heart through maturity and conviction no doubt brought about the reformed behavior. Not stopping there, he also removed the final remnant of sodomites out of the land (1 Kgs. 22:46). So for all of the good that he did, God established him and gave him abundant honor and riches. (2 Chr. 17:5)

One also reads of Jehoshaphat joining evil King Ahab of Israel in battle against Syria. In this complex account, the Bible pronounces his discernment and humility before God as he discounts the false predictions of Ahab's "hand-picked" false prophets. Jehoshaphat humbly insists on hearing the real Words of God before entering into a serious battle (1 Kgs. 22:5-8). It was in this battle that Ahab lost his life. But while Jehoshaphat's life was spared, he was nevertheless judged for his compromise with men of evil.

> *And Jehu the son of Hanani the seer went out to meet*
> *him, and said to king Jehoshaphat, Shouldest thou help*
> *the ungodly, and love them that hate the LORD?*
> *therefore is wrath upon thee from before the LORD. (2*
> *Chr. 19:2)*

Sometime thereafter, fearing a difficult battle with the Ammonites and Moabites, Jehoshaphat again returns to his humble state by proclaiming a fast (2 Chr. 20:3) and by leading Judah in bowing to the ground and worshipping God (2 Chr. 20:18). Surprisingly, even after these acts of humility before God, driven by fear (pride), he makes another alliance with evil. This second allegiance is with evil

King Ahaziah of Israel and receives an almost identical rebuke as before:

> *Then Eliezer the son of Dodavah of Mareshah prophesied against Jehoshaphat, saying, Because thou hast joined thyself with Ahaziah, the LORD hath broken thy works. And the ships were broken, that they were not able to go to Tarshish. (2 Chr. 20:37)*

It appears that shortly after this second incident, Jehoshaphat's days are shortened similar to his great-great grandfather.

King Manasseh

Some one hundred sixty years later, the Bible tells of a certain King of Judah who displayed pride and wickedness throughout much of his life. Manasseh, who became king at age twelve and reigned for fifty-five years:

> *did that which was evil in the sight of the LORD, after the abominations of the heathen, whom the LORD cast out before the children of Israel. (2 Kgs. 21:2)*

Part of the irony of Manasseh's record is that he was the son of King Hezekiah who did many good things in the sight of the Lord (18:3). This behavior disproves the secular adage: "the apple doesn't fall far from the tree." He cannot even use the excuse that he was only twelve when he began to reign since his father became king at age eight. Regarding Manasseh's evil pride, Second Kings 21 discloses that he specifically built "high places" of occultic worship, set graven images throughout Judah, built altars of idolatry to Baal in the House of the Lord, practiced witchcraft, observed superstitions, summoned demons, shed much innocent blood, and even conducted burning sacrifices of children that included one of his very sons. Not only did Manasseh partake in these heinous acts, but the Bible asserts that he seduced other Jews to participate more so than the heathen nations (2 Chr. 33:9). If that were not enough, extra-Biblical accounts state that Manasseh had the humble prophet Isaiah sawn into two pieces.

It is here, for the first time in the Old Testament, that God communicates His complete disapproval of Judah and His plan to utterly punish them:

> *Because Manasseh king of Judah hath done these abominations, and hath done wickedly above all that the Amorites did, which were before him, and hath made Judah also to sin with his idols: Therefore thus saith the LORD God of Israel, Behold, I am bringing such evil upon Jerusalem and Judah, that whosoever heareth of it, both his ears shall tingle. (2 Kgs. 21:11-12)*

God's longsuffering nature towards His chosen people delayed the execution of punishment for approximately one hundred ten years from this pronouncement. At that point in time (586 B.C.), God built and stirred the adversary of Babylonia to dispense His righteous punishment through the captivity of Jerusalem and the first *diaspora*. The impact of this ultimate punishment is still being felt today by Jews worldwide.

Now comes the most marvelous part of Manasseh's story. As a means to bring low the king's haughtiness, the Lord enabled Assyrian captains to take Manasseh to Babylon in chains. Once in Babylon, it appears that the king humbles himself and experiences a miraculous conversion that transformed his previously wicked heart:

> *And when he was in affliction, he besought the LORD his God, and humbled himself greatly before the God of his fathers, And prayed unto him: and he was intreated of him, and heard his supplication, and brought him again to Jerusalem into his kingdom. Then Manasseh knew that the LORD he was God...And he took away the strange gods, and the idol out of the house of the LORD, and all the altars that he had built in the mount of the house of the LORD, and in Jerusalem, and cast them out of the city. And he repaired the altar of the LORD, and sacrificed thereon peace offerings and thank offerings, and commanded Judah to serve the LORD God of Israel. (2 Chr. 33:12-13,15-16)*

What makes this a true heart conversion is that Manasseh returns to Jerusalem and enacts sweeping reform.

Not just in one area of his life but in several. He was not just caught in the emotion of being imprisoned in a strange land. There was conviction and outward manifestations of his "new found" belief. It is likely that Manasseh learned about the Lord from his father since Hezekiah was alive for his first nine years of kingship. This account should encourage parents of teen and adult children that are not walking with the Lord as it reaffirms the Biblical truth:

> *Train up a child in the way he should go: and when he is old, he will not depart from it. (Prov. 22:6)*

Nebuchadnezzar

A fascinating account of how displays of humility are fleeting without true faith and a relationship with God comes from Babylonian King Nebuchadnezzar. This Biblical "roller-coaster" of pride and humility commences with his plundering and eventual destruction of Jerusalem. Those that survived the onslaught of pestilence, famine and sword were brought back to Babylon as captives. Only a small remnant was left in Judah as vinedressers and husbandmen. Second Chronicles graphically depicts the conquest and the king's underlying haughtiness:

> *Therefore he brought upon them the king of the Chaldees, who slew their young men with the sword in the house of their sanctuary, and had no compassion upon young man or maiden, old man, or him that stooped for age: he gave them all into his hand. And all the vessels of the house of God, great and small, and the treasures of the house of the LORD, and the treasures of the king, and of his princes; all these he brought to Babylon. And they burnt the house of God, and brake down the wall of Jerusalem, and burnt all the palaces thereof with fire, and destroyed all the goodly vessels thereof. And them that had escaped from the sword carried he away to Babylon; where they were servants to him and his sons until the reign of the kingdom of Persia: To fulfil the word of the LORD by the mouth of Jeremiah, until the land had enjoyed her sabbaths: for as long as she lay desolate she kept*

sabbath, to fulfil threescore and ten years. (2 Chron. 36:17-21)

Although the Lord was one hundred percent behind the act, Nebuchadnezzar no doubt believed that his abilities were the sole cause of this victory.

Notwithstanding, turning to the book of Daniel, one sees that Nebuchadnezzar makes generous provisions to prominent Hebrew captives: Daniel, Hananiah, Mishael, and Azariah (Dan. 1:3-5). Because of Daniel's wisdom, the King became especially appreciative and close with the prophet (Dan. 1:19-21). The Bible subsequently tells of Daniel knowing and accurately interpreting Nebuchadnezzar's private dream. (Dan. 2:26-45) It is at this point that readers experience the ruler's first round humility as he falls to worship Daniel:

> *"The king answered unto Daniel, and said, Of a truth it is, that your God is a God of gods, and a Lord of kings, and a revealer of secrets, seeing thou couldest reveal this secret." (Daniel 2:47)*

Even after this glorious miracle and the appointment of Shadrach, Meshach and Abednego, Nebuchadnezzar takes a turn for the worse. The Bible next tells of him building and dedicating a gold statue of himself for all to revere. The monarch even institutes a "fiery furnace" penalty for those that do not comply. Nebuchadnezzar then makes a boastful and blasphemous statement to non-compliant Shadrach, Meshach, and Abednego: *"...who is that God that shall deliver you out of my hands?"* (3:15) Things get worse as he also becomes furious and completely changes his demeanor towards the three men. It is here where the Bible presents the familiar record of Jesus Christ accompanying and preserving the three from a deathly incineration (3:21-27). Amazed by this miraculous intervention, Nebuchadnezzar proclaims,

> *"...Blessed be the God of Shadrach, Meshach, and Abednego, who hath sent his angel, and delivered his servants that trusted in him, and have changed the king's word, and yielded their bodies, that they might not*

serve nor worship any god, except their own God."
(Daniel 3:28)

He rightly humbles himself before God and decrees that no one should speak against God. Disobedience would result in being cut into pieces. He even promotes the wise men into prominent roles. In Daniel chapter four, he goes on to state,

"How great are his signs! and how mighty are his wonders! his kingdom is an everlasting kingdom, and his dominion is from generation to generation." (Daniel 4:3)

On all fronts, it appears that Nebuchadnezzar is a new man. He now has been exposed to two miracles and appears to have entirely repented. Unfortunately, the Bible reveals that pride was still deeply rooted in his heart. After being told by Daniel (through a second dream interpretation) that he would lose his kingdom and undergo degradation unless he repent (4:27), Nebuchadnezzar does one prideful act and speaks another. He first arrogantly ignores Daniel's prophecy by not altering his behavior for twelve months. He then makes one of the most boastful "I" statements found in God's Words. He says,

"... Is not this great Babylon, that I have built for the house of the kingdom by the might of my power, and for the honour of my majesty?" (Dan. 4:30)

Unbelievably, he revisits the heaping of glory upon himself. How many have also experienced moments of deep lowness and submission to God only to return to arrogance and haughtiness? Vows and promises to follow God are made during the trial but in a little while the old ways return as soon as things calm down. Despair not, as God will always lift-up those who turn to Him, regardless of the situation. This is exactly what Nebuchadnezzar did after his humiliating exile:

And at the end of the days I Nebuchadnezzar lifted up mine eyes unto heaven, and mine understanding returned unto me, and I blessed the most High, and I praised and honoured him that liveth for ever, whose

> *dominion is an everlasting dominion, and his kingdom is*
> *from generation to generation: (Daniel 4:34)*

Almighty God then fully restores the once mad and banished regent to the point of adding "excellent majesty" to his authority. Nebuchadnezzar recites his final Biblical words in meek God-honoring fashion:

> *"Now I Nebuchadnezzar praise and extol and honour the*
> *King of heaven, all whose works are truth, and his ways*
> *judgment: and those that walk in pride he is able to*
> *abase." (Daniel 4:37)*

Daniel correspondingly makes mention of the ruler's Godly finish.

> *..till he knew that the most high God ruled in the kingdom*
> *of men, and that he appointeth over it whomsoever he*
> *will. (Daniel 5:21)*

A Christian should desire to end their life so well.

Simon Peter

The final ensample of a character that illustrated both pride and humility comes from the Apostle Simon Peter. While Peter mostly demonstrated meekness and lowliness, there are a few noteworthy exceptions, especially prior to Pentecost. As such, it is best to divide Cephas' life into three distinct periods: pre-crucifixion, post-crucifixion to ascension, and Pentecost onward.

Pre-Crucifixion Life

Studying the pre-crucifixion period, one discovers that Peter was humbly obedient to Jesus' directives. He left his nets (livelihood) to follow Messiah (Matt. 4:19-20), fell down at Jesus' knees after doubting that the nets would fill-up with fish (Luke 5:8), wanted Christ to wash him head-to-toe (John 13:9), and believed that the Lord Jesus had the words of eternal life calling Christ the "Son of the living God" (Matt. 16:16; John 6:68-69). Peter also was only one of two disciples that chose to follow Jesus to the High Priest's Palace during the initial phase of the "Passion" (John 18:15). Contrarily, several overt displays of pride and vanity throughout this time frame are observed. Christ strongly rebuked Peter for offending God's will and for preferring things of man over things of God. Matthew's Gospel pronounces,

> *"Then Peter took him, and began to rebuke him, saying, Be it far from thee, Lord: this shall not be unto thee. But he turned, and said unto Peter, Get thee behind me, Satan: thou art an offence unto me: for thou savourest not the things that be of God, but those that be of men."* *(16:22-23).*

It also appears that Peter was conveying a form of flattery to Christ. Soon thereafter, the Gospel of Matthew also discloses how Jesus corrected Peter's hasty response about paying custom or tribute:

> *...What thinkest thou, Simon? of whom do the kings of the earth take custom or tribute? of their own children, or of strangers? (Matt. 17:25)*

One also reads about how Peter (and other disciples) selfishly valued sleep over prayer and vigilance during the final critical moments in the Garden of Gethsemane (Matt. 26:40; Mark 14:37).

The last and most infamous of all of Peter's prideful displays is found in the thrice denial of Christ. Predicted by Christ, the denials became a stark depiction of how people who profess belief in Christ will disown Him in the face of real persecution. After Peter falsely avowed (during relative calm) never to be offended because of Him, Jesus answered him,

> *"Wilt thou lay down thy life for my sake? Verily, verily, I say unto thee, The cock shall not crow, till thou hast denied me thrice." (John. 13:38)*

It soon became apparent that Simon was not willing to even ruin his reputation much less his life.

> *And Peter remembered the word of Jesus, which said unto him, Before the cock crow, thou shalt deny me thrice. And he went out, and wept bitterly. (Matt. 26:75)*

Fortunately for Peter, God subsequently bestowed on him a second opportunity to give all to Jesus Christ. Not all may be so blessed to receive a second chance since no one knows their appointed time to die as life on earth is but a brief vapour (Jas. 4:14). Meditating on the denial verses, will people truly sacrifice themselves for Christ? Sacrificing for the cause of Christ is happening today across the world as true born-again disciples are forced to give up their jobs, their home, their security, their children, and even their lives. (The organization "Voice of the Martyrs" does a faithful job in presenting true chronicles of modern-day saints who would rather die than to deny Christ.) This could very well be what separates a false convert from a regenerated believer. This is reminiscent of the story of two men who walk into a Sunday church service with loaded shotguns. They angrily yell, "anyone who is not willing to take a bullet for Christ leave now!" The once three hundred person filled sanctuary starts emptying. First, most of the people in the pews, then two-thirds of the choir followed by half of the deacons, leaving only the pastor with thirty or so left in the whole building. At that point, the gunmen put away their shotguns and politely say, "Ok Pastor, please re-commence your sermon as the hypocrites are gone now." Are we true believers or are we hypocrites; false converts? Ask God to search your heart and if a shred of doubt exists, pray, repent and ask God for forgiveness. Then you must restate your belief and commitment to Christ!

Post-Crucifixion Life

The fifty days post crucifixion, Peter demonstrates an improved and mostly humble demeanor. Not yet possessing the power of the Holy Spirit (still working through the flesh), Peter demonstrated humility by unashamedly running to the sepulchre upon hearing of the absence of Christ's body (Luke 24:12), immediately jumping with joy and anticipation into the water to meet the resurrected Christ at the shore (John 21:7), and thrice expressing his love for Jesus. This verse in John 21 states:

> *He saith unto him the third time, Simon, son of Jonas, lovest thou me? Peter was grieved because he said unto him the third time, Lovest thou me? And he said unto him, Lord, thou knowest all things; thou knowest that I love thee. Jesus saith unto him, Feed my sheep." (John 21:17)*

Christ asking the same question three times was a plain allusion to Peter denying Him three times only weeks earlier. The one conspicuous act of pride during this brief interlude comes when Peter asked Christ about how John would be used as a believer and how he would die (John 21:20-21). This question may have been a continuation of the apostle's discussion on who would be the greatest in the kingdom. At the very least, it is comparative, which mostly indicates the existence of pride. Regardless of Peter's true motivation, Christ, knowing his heart, responds,

> *"...If I will that he tarry till I come, what is that to thee? follow thou me." (John. 21:22)*

It seems that Christ was telling Peter to simply follow him and not to concern himself with how John will die or how he will be used. Glorious words to live by!

Pentecost and Beyond

After receiving the Holy Ghost at Pentecost, one reads of Peter's fearless leadership (Acts 1:15; 8:20) and selfless zeal for preaching and seeing lost souls saved (2:14-41; 10:44). Peter's humility is also expressed by him giving God the glory (3:6, 12; 4:19; 10:26), having unwavering obedience (5:29), establishing believer's baptism for the church (2:41; 10:48), healing (5:5; 9:34), and miraculously resurrecting a dead woman named Tabitha (9:39-41). Peter was also mightily used by God to remove the "yoke" of circumcision as a perceived prerequisite for salvation (15:7-11). Christians must make strong note of the grace by which Peter spoke in order to convince those of the early church that thought otherwise. This would have been unlikely years earlier.

The Apostle Peter's only occurrence of pride post-Pentecost was uncovered by none other than the Apostle Paul. More than likely imperceptible to the undiscerning heart, Paul blames Peter for behaving differently toward Gentile Christians depending on the presence or not of Jewish Christians (Gal. 2:11-14). Paul also notices that other Jewish Christians (even Barnabas) are behaving likewise, quite possibly influenced by Peter's leadership. Paul aptly calls this behavior dissimulation which can be also called hypocritical pride.

Ending on an encouraging note, Peter's teachings on humility are still foundational to Christian living and doctrine. The two passages that best exemplify this truth are:

> *Likewise, ye younger, submit yourselves unto the elder. Yea, all of you be subject one to another, and be clothed with humility: for God resisteth the proud, and giveth grace to the humble. Humble yourselves therefore under the mighty hand of God, that he may exalt you in due time. (1 Pet. 5:5-6)*

> *But grow in grace, and in the knowledge of our Lord and Saviour Jesus Christ. To him be glory both now and for ever. Amen. (2 Pet. 3:18)*

Simon Peter provides an example that millions have been able to identify with as it projects a very imperfect man prior to receiving the indwelling of the Holy Spirit. Once receiving the Holy Spirit, the power of God through Peter's many words and acts are witnessed. Although the office of Apostle and its powers (laying the doctrinal foundations of the church, resurrecting the dead etc.) have ceased, it should still be a believer's heart desire to possess the zeal for God, fearless love of evangelism and desire for doctrinal purity that Peter exuded!

CHAPTER 16

HUMBLING AND SEX

Introduction

The Bible touches several times on a very sensitive topic. It is the topic of being sexually "humbled." While all of these Scriptures specifically address men shaming women, many men could also be impacted through the humbling of their wife, daughters, sisters or mother. On two occasions, men and male angels were nearly humbled themselves by other men. However, as one looks closer at the specific verses below, it is readily identifiable that the Words of God not only consider the forcible act of rape as humbling or shaming but also deems any illicit (not sanctioned by God) sexual exploit as an act of humbling. As such, consensual adult sex would still be considered an act of humbling if committed outside of God's directives.

An Example From Genesis: Dinah

One first reads of sexual humbling in the book of Genesis as Shechem forcibly takes Dinah, the daughter of Jacob. Grippingly, this is not the typical rape that is portrayed by the media and feminists of today. The Bible states that Shechem actually loved Dinah and wanted to marry her. Those facts not-withstanding, it was still an act of force that was not sanctioned by God through Jacob. It was a dehumanizing act that defiled Dinah. Even some of her brothers said, "Should he (Shechem) deal with our sister as with an harlot" (34:31)? Picking-up the account in Genesis 34:1, Moses writes:

> *And Dinah the daughter of Leah, which she bare unto Jacob, went out to see the daughters of the land. And when Shechem the son of Hamor the Hivite, prince of the country, saw her, he took her, and lay with her, and defiled her. And his soul clave unto Dinah the daughter of Jacob, and he loved the damsel, and spake kindly*

unto the damsel. And Shechem spake unto his father Hamor, saying, Get me this damsel to wife. (Vs. 1-4)

The record goes on to note that Shechem even implored his father (Hamor) to beg Jacob to make Dinah his wife. Jacob and his sons would have none of it as Shechem and Hamor (who condoned the act) were soon recompensed at the blades of Simeon and Levi (34:25-26).

Three Examples From Deuteronomy

The book of Deuteronomy also contains three mentions of sexual humbling. The first one specifies laws for wives captured in battle:

And it shall be, if thou have no delight in her, then thou shalt let her go whither she will; but thou shalt not sell her at all for money, thou shalt not make merchandise of her, because thou hast humbled her. (Deut. 21:14)

The second deliberates the consequence of a bethrothed virgin who commits adultery with a man not to be her husband:

Then ye shall bring them both out unto the gate of that city, and ye shall stone them with stones that they die; the damsel, because she cried not, being in the city; and the man, because he hath humbled his neighbour's wife: so thou shalt put away evil from among you. (Deut. 22:24)

The third mention is a continuation of the above verse and declares that a man who sexually humbles another woman must pay her father silver as reparation and, additionally, cannot throw her out (Deut. 22:29). These last two mentions are interesting given the rampant promiscuity in "post-modern" cultures. Very few today would conceive that humbling or lowering oneself would occur from simply having unmarried sex with another adult.

Example From Ezekiel

Another illustration of sexual humbling is found in the book of Ezekiel. The prophet writes:

In thee have they discovered their fathers' nakedness: in thee have they humbled her that was set apart for pollution. And one hath committed abomination with his neighbour's wife; and another hath lewdly defiled his daughter in law; and another in thee hath humbled his sister, his father's daughter. (22:10-11)

Growing Debauchery

This passage also addresses the non-sanctioned sex that wretchedly has taken place between relatives. As experts have warned for years, the slippery slope of allowing sinful homosexual marriage has now moved onto individuals contesting the courts to marry their parents, children or siblings. Others are disputing the legal age of marriage, hoping to disgustingly marry young boys or girls. Others are challenging for their right to create three and four-way marriages. Nothing is sacred as some have spoken about marrying their much-loved pets. Their familiar mantras are: "We're in love,"; "We're not hurting anybody,"; "Why are you trying to prevent me from being happy?"; and the all too common "You're a hater!". As absolute morality gets replaced by "anything goes" relativism, society will be thrust into once unthinkable situations. If the Lord tarries, given the rate of decay, it is not beyond the realm of possibility that all marriage boundaries will cease to exist in the lifetimes of today's living adults.

An Example From Judges

The final mention of sexual humbling comes from Judges 19. It is a strange record of an evil group of Gibeonites who initially wanted to homosexually rape a travelling Levite but eventually settled on vilely abusing (humbling) his concubine all night long. As a side note, it is interesting that the concubine had previously played the harlot with other men against her husband, cited in verse two. The lewd account states:

Behold, here is my daughter a maiden, and his concubine; them I will bring out now, and humble ye them, and do with them what seemeth good unto you: but unto this man do not so vile a thing. But the men would not hearken to him: so the man took his concubine, and brought her forth unto them; and they knew her, and abused her all the night until the morning: and when the day began to spring, they let her go. (Jdg. 19:24-25)

After the husband rises (Unbelievably, it appears he was able to rest comfortably inside!) the concubine is found dead outside from the abuse. The account now sounds almost like a Satanic Hollywood horror movie as the Levite proceeds to cut the concubine into twelve pieces and sends a piece of her to a representative of each of the twelve tribes. It appears the husband wanted all to know of the atrocity that was done by these men that lived within Benjamin. This act so enraged the eleven other tribes that after a series of events they rose up in civil war against Benjamin. Hence, this act of perversion, abuse, and violence almost led to the complete destruction of one of the twelve tribes!

The "Why?" Question

Some may ask, why does God allow this and other sorts of humbling in the lives of people? Some may respond,

> "Humiliation represents the humbling experiences that God brings into our lives to destroy the sin of pride and to help us develop Godly humility."[75]

Others may simply say that one should accept with gratitude everything that God allows in order to be reminded of the need for humbling.

The Answer

The Biblical truth is that God allows bad things to occur in order to prove, sanctify, and know what is in the hearts of His people. About this very subject, the Apostle Peter writes,

---

[75] Wayne Mack, <u>Humility: The Forgotten Virtue</u> (Phillipsburg, NJ: P&R Publishing, 2005), 19.

> *"That the trial of your faith, being much more precious than of gold that perisheth, though it be tried with fire, might be found unto praise and honour and glory at the appearing of Jesus Christ." (1 Pet. 1:7)*

The Apostle Paul tackled the same matter:

> *And lest, when I come again, my God will humble me among you, and that I shall bewail many which have sinned already, and have not repented of the uncleanness and fornication and lasciviousness which they have committed. (2 Cor. 12:21)*

The tragic or evil storms of life will always come. When this happens in the life of a saint, he should always strive to have the attitude and speech of Joseph. Even after he was ridiculed, ostracized, thrown into a pit, and sold into slavery by his brothers; even after he was falsely accused and thrown into prison; even after he had not seen his beloved father, Jacob, and his younger brother, Benjamin, for many years; this is what he had to say,

> *"But as for you, ye thought evil against me; but God meant it unto good, to bring to pass, as it is this day, to save much people alive." (Gen. 50:20)*

The final meditation is that God allows certain things to occur in people's lives to draw them to Him. Often, "bad" experiences give the recipients a special appreciation for what God and Jesus Christ have done. God providentially chooses some to help those that are in comparable trials. Often, there may only be one person in a congregation that can minister to certain hurts and despairs. It is one of the reasons that believers come together as a body: *"Not forsaking the assembling of ourselves together, as the manner of some is; but exhorting one another: and so much the more, as ye see the day approaching."* (Heb. 10:25)

CHAPTER 17

FALSE HUMILITY

At this point, a brief examination of "False Humility" is necessary because it is all too often confused with true God-honoring humility to the undiscerning eye and ear. *False humility is nothing less than a very subtle form of pride*. It seeks to make the manipulator appear contrary to his true motivation. It can even bring about a form a self-delusion in thinking that someone is really humble, when they are actually the opposite. Even the mature saint is tested in identifying its manifestation as the Scriptures warn of ministers of Satan posing as righteous servants of God.

> *Therefore it is no great thing if his ministers also be transformed as the ministers of righteousness; whose end shall be according to their works. (2 Cor. 11:15)*

Examples

Moses

Returning to Moses, some scholars cite that he exhibited false humility when he protested to God that he was a poor speaker and couldn't do the job asked of him. Exodus chapter four presents the account:

> *And Moses said unto the LORD, O my Lord, I am not eloquent, neither heretofore, nor since thou hast spoken unto thy servant: but I am slow of speech, and of a slow tongue. (Exod. 4:10)*

Even after God assured Moses that He would teach him what to speak, Moses asked for additional assistance (Exod. 4:11). At this point, Moses (through his false humility) provokes God's anger, prompting the insertion of Aaron for aid. One can conclude that Moses' persistent rebuttals to God actually contradicted his point of being slow of speech and tongue. In addition, while man cannot judge Moses' true heart condition, one is able to witness, in the Bible, how Moses artfully debated with Pharaoh, articulated to God why He should spare the Israelites from complete destruction in the wilderness, and delivered inspirational oratories to mass Israelite gatherings. All of these lend credence to the position that Moses was displaying an understated form of pride; but pride nevertheless.

The Pharisees

The quintessential passage on false humility however comes directly from our Lord Jesus Christ. Speaking in parables, Christ confronts the Pharisees and others who are like them by stating,

> *"The Pharisee stood and prayed thus with himself, God, I thank thee, that I am not as other men are, extortioners, unjust, adulterers, or even as this publican. I fast twice in the week, I give tithes of all that I possess."*
> *(Luke. 18:11-12)*

Here the Lord provides an example of false humility through prayer and worship. Pride shows itself clearly through its comparative nature as well as through the expounding of all the "good" done in life. Thus, it can be said:

> "Pride can clothe itself in the garments of praise or of penitence…Pride can lift its head in the very temple of God and make His worship the scene of self-exaltation."[76]

In the rest of the passage, the Lord contrasts the Pharisee with the truly humble publican who is filled with repentance and basically understands his low position before God. His prayers have power since Christ promised that he will be exalted for his lowliness.

False Humility Warnings

In the book of Colossians, Paul also warns on the matter of false or voluntary humility:

> *Let no man beguile you of your reward in a voluntary humility and worshipping of angels, intruding into those*

---

[76] Andrew Murray, <u>Humility</u> (New Kensington, PA: Whitaker, 1982), 68-69.

things which he hath not seen, vainly puffed up by his fleshly mind." (Col. 2:18)

A couple of truths can be exposited from this verse. One is that this "voluntary" humility is beguiling. It appears authentic. Paul is, in essence, conveying that this act is nothing more than a well-executed counterfeit.

One also reads of its connection to vanity, haughtiness and a mind that believes it is smarter than all others around it. A few verses later, Paul continuing the theme pens:

Which things have indeed a shew of wisdom in will worship, and humility, and neglecting of the body; not in any honour to the satisfying of the flesh. (Col. 2:23).

Modest clothing, soft words, inauspicious living, fasting etc. can be marks of false humility as they can disguise even the proudest of hearts. More obvious forms of false humility are flagrant acts of self-loathing or self-flagellation since it is still about self.

"Being occupied with self, even amid the deepest self-abhorrence, can never free us from self."[77]

Close fellowship and trials still appear to be two of the more effective means of exposing of false humility.

Another area of false humility comes from not having an opinion. This form of "straddling the fence" desires never to offend or to be everyone's friend. To the unbeliever, this behavior is described as being agreeable or affable. Deceitfully labeled as "tolerance," it has been pushed as a "virtue" by secularists for many years. Today's society has pejoratively named it, "Political Correctness," as it is frequently embraced by politicians and people trying to create self-gain. The King James Bible calls people who engage in this type of behavior as menpleasers (Eph. 6:6; Col. 3:22) as they are gripped with moral relativism. *At a distance, even to born-again believers, this appears to be a*

---

[77] Ibid., 80.

manifestation of "grace." However, upon close inspection, it is not grace that is operating but rather a lack of grounded convictions or beliefs. It can be oxymoronically termed as "Christian Relativism." (A recent example of this comes from Pastor Joel Osteen who either from his incomplete knowledge of Scriptures or through his desire not to offend anyone has publicly declared that Mormons are Christians. A more sinister reason may be at work but we should let the Lord decide if this is the case.) *Thus, it can be rightly said that false humility is refusing to take a stance on what one considers to be truth.*

The final view of voluntary humility expounds that man prays for humility in word, but in his secret heart he wants to be kept from the things that will make him humble. It has already been verified Biblically that events and circumstances that can humble people are normally painful; and rarely does anyone pray for that.

CHAPTER 18

JESUS CHRIST:
OUR ULTIMATE EXAMPLE

True Humility and the Lord Jesus Christ

The last example of humility and meekness is found in the greatest example; through the Lord Jesus Christ. Probing deeper, not only is Christ's humility the utmost ensample, but it is the only one that allows for all other manifestations of true humility. Without Christ's atoning sacrificial death and resurrection, the Holy Spirit's power to convict, transform and comfort would not constantly abide within man. True conversion and regeneration (being born-again) would not be possible. Thus, as believers grow in Christ, their acts of modesty flow from being a new creature and not from a self-deluded and camouflaged self-serving nature. In all other religions and in some apostate Christian denominations, acts of charity stem from satisfying their god(s) and/or doctrine. Since it is ultimately not rooted in being a "new" person but rather in doctrinal appeasement, it translates itself into feeling proud about one's good deeds. With true Christianity, Christ and humility are inextricably bound:

> "Christ's humility is our salvation. Christ's salvation is our humility."[78]

Suffice to say that sundry books can be written solely about this subject. At present, the review will just briefly touch on the subject and save the deeper study for another occasion, Lord permitting.

True Humility and the Incarnation

First, addressing the humility of Jesus Christ in His incarnation, John chapter one states:

---

[78] Andrew Murray, <u>Humility</u> (New Kensington, PA: Whitaker, 1982), 17.

> *In the beginning was the Word, and the Word was with God, and the Word was God. The same was in the beginning with God. All things were made by him; and without him was not any thing made that was made. (John 1:1-3)*

Paul, in the Epistle to Hebrews, also writes:

> *And, Thou, Lord, in the beginning hast laid the foundation of the earth; and the heavens are the works of thine hands. (Hebrews 1:10)*

From these passages, it is clear that Christ not only existed from the beginning (not a creation) but was wholly part of the creating. This truth was also revealed by Jesus Christ himself:

> *And now, O Father, glorify thou me with thine own self with the glory which I had with thee before the world was. (John 17:5)*

Hence, being very God, Christ became very man. He would leave heaven to experience a human existence filled with the common emotions of joy, pain, tiredness, sorrow, etc. Most would consider this a serious demotion; a downgrade in status. So why did He do it? Christ Himself informs humanity of the overarching reason:

> *For I came down from heaven, not to do mine own will, but the will of him that sent me...And this is the will of him that sent me, that every one which seeth the Son, and believeth on him, may have everlasting life: and I will raise him up at the last day. (John. 6:38, 40)*

Christ also humbly informs us that the doctrines He teaches are of the Father and are not His (John 7:16). One of the passages that best illustrates Christ's humility in being made flesh is found in the Philippian epistle. Here Paul expands on the Lord's incomprehensible act of lowliness:

> *Who, being in the form of God, thought it not robbery to be equal with God: But made himself of no reputation, and took upon him the form of a servant, and was made in the likeness of men: And being found in fashion as a*

man, he humbled himself, and became obedient unto
death, even the death of the cross. (Phil. 2:6-8)

Just from Christ's incarnation one can rightly conclude that pride is foolish because of how our Saviour emptied himself, took on a servant nature, and was obedient to the Father. It would be convincing enough if these were His only manifestations of humility, yet there are several more to consider.

True Humility and the Lord's Daily Life

The Lord's daily life and decisions conveyed the epitome of humility. While humbling Himself before His creatures, Scripture notes that Christ was meek and lowly of heart (Matt. 11:29), was just and lowly (Zech. 9:9), meek (sitting upon a colt) (Mark 11:7), was meek and gentle (2 Cor. 10:1), submitted to the Father's will (John 4:34; 8:28, 29), came to do the Father's will, not His (John 6:38), did nothing by Himself (John 8:28), did not seek His own glory (John 8:50), was devoted to glorifying the Father (John 17:1-4), came to serve others (Luke 22:27; Mark 10:45), came to minister (Matt. 20:28), washed His disciple's feet (John 13), and though rich became poor (2 Cor. 8:9). During His three year ministry, Christ also humbly demonstrated many healing miracles. *The four Gospels record Christ enacting thirty-six unique miracles over the laws of nature which He created.* These miracles gave great multitudes joy and hope. The unembellished reality is that Jesus touched countless more people than the thirty-six documented miracles attest to as written by John the Beloved:

And there are also many other things which Jesus did,
the which, if they should be written every one, I suppose
that even the world itself could not contain the books that
should be written. Amen. (John. 21:25)

Thus, there can be no doubt that Jesus Christ was as humble in His fellowship with men as He was with the Father. He considered Himself a servant of men.

True Humility: Speaking Boldly and Honestly

Through His meekness and humility, Christ also demonstrated courage to speak boldly and honestly. He most certainly spoke often of the judgment of hell and of not repenting of sins:

And shall cast them into a furnace of fire: there shall be wailing and gnashing of teeth. (Matt. 13:42);

And these shall go away into everlasting punishment: but the righteous into life eternal." (Matt. 25:46) "I tell you, Nay: but, except ye repent, ye shall all likewise perish. (Luke. 13:3; Matt. 8:12; 22:13; 24:51; 25:46; Luke 13:28)

Similarly, Christ warned about the consequence of not putting Him first:

He that loveth father or mother more than me is not worthy of me: and he that loveth son or daughter more than me is not worthy of me."(Matt. 10:37).

Mostly ignored by liberal ecumenical teachers, Christ also declared that He would bring division not peace. Luke the Physician cites the most complete rendering of this passage:

Suppose ye that I am come to give peace on earth? I tell you, Nay; but rather division: For from henceforth there shall be five in one house divided, three against two, and two against three. The father shall be divided against the son, and the son against the father; the mother against the daughter, and the daughter against the mother; the mother in law against her daughter in law, and the daughter in law against her mother in law. (12:51-53)

Likewise, He declared that true believers will hate (relative to the love they have for Christ) their father, mother (Luke 14:26) and the world (John 12:25).

Other seemingly hard but yet still meek sayings of Christ are when He called Jewish priests evil, hypocrites and serpents (Matt. 16:6; 22:18; 23:33; Mark 7:6; Luke 11:39; 13:15), declared that blasphemy against the Holy Spirit would not be forgiven (Matt. 12:31; Mark 3:29), required the keeping of the commandments (Matt. 19:18; Mark 10:19; Luke 18:20), denied the existence of purgatory (Luke 16:19-31), decreed the hanging and drowning of child offenders (Mark 9:42; Luke 17:2), called Peter the evil one…Satan (Mark 8:33), condemned divorce (Mark 10:11-12), said to His mother, *"Woman, what have I to do with thee? mine hour is not yet come"* (John 2:4), and called the Jews of the day faithless and perverse (Mark 9:19; Luke 9:41). What makes these "tough" declarations of Christ humble and not mean or arrogant? It is because they were all true statements that were meant to bring unbelievers to repentance and to bring the regenerated disciple to maturity. Since He created man, He knew what was best for him. Otherwise, man would be left to decide for himself what is right and wrong. As discussed previously, humankind is presently experiencing the societal decay that is surging from the current absence of moral absolutism.

True Humility and Jesus' Teachings

Not only did Jesus the Christ live by humble example, He also imparted various teachings on the theme of lowliness and meekness. The Messiah taught that self-abasement would allow for the blessings of heaven and earth (Matt. 5:3-5), would bring greatness in the kingdom (Matt. 18:4; Luke 9:48), was the only way to honor (Matt. 23:11), and would lead to exaltation (Luke 14:11). Christ also instructed that meekness will enable perfect rest for the soul (Matt. 11:29), that the chief will be the servant (Matt. 20:27-28), and to always worship in humility (Luke 18:14).

By teaching that one must become a servant of others, Christ instructed that humility is not just a form of meditation. It involves works and actions. Many verses outline this eternal teaching of which additional interpretation would only take away from the Son's Words. Here are just a few of them. Christ commenced the Sermon on the Mount by saying,

> *"Blessed are the poor in spirit: for theirs is the kingdom of heaven." (Matt. 5:3)*

After the disciples proudly disputed who would be the greatest in the kingdom, Jesus said to them,

> *"...Whosoever shall receive this child in my name receiveth me: and whosoever shall receive me receiveth him that sent me: for he that is least among you all, the same shall be great." (Luke. 9:48)*

At the Lord's Supper, the disciples still disputed who would be great. The Lord's retort this time was,

> *"But ye shall not be so: but he that is greatest among you, let him be as the younger; and he that is chief, as he that doth serve." (Luke. 22:26)*

Christ gave instructions after washing His disciple's feet.

> *If I then, your Lord and Master, have washed your feet; ye also ought to wash one another's feet. (John 13:14)*

Lastly, speaking to the multitudes about the Pharisees' desiring seats of honor, Christ said,

> *"But he that is greatest among you shall be your servant." (Matt. 23:11)*

The plain Scriptural truth is that saints are commanded to be humble. If we are commanded to do so then it implies a choice; a responsibility. This command is for the well-being of the disciple, for the good of others, and for the pleasure of God. When one is truly at his lowest, God promises to exalt. God's merciful and righteous exaltation of humble mankind is beautifully articulated by another Andrew Murray quote:

> Look to it that you abase and humble yourselves, and take no place before God or man but that of servant; that is your work; let that be your one purpose and prayer. God is faithful. Just as water ever seeks and fills the lowest place, so the moment God finds the creature abased and empty, His glory and power flow in to exalt and to bless.[79]

---

[79] Andrew Murray, <u>Humility</u> (New Kensington, PA: Whitaker, 1982), 70.

CHAPTER 19

IS HUMILITY POSSIBLE TODAY?

The Answer is Yes

Even though flawless Christ-like humility is impossible for saints to realize, God would not command something that was not possible to attain. Not making humility possible would make God a liar and Biblicists know from His eternal Words that He is righteous and immutable. Nevertheless, the fact that humility is attainable does not make it a virtue that is easily achieved.

The Stumbling Blocks to True Humility

The Thirteen "E's"

The Prince of the Power of the Air has from the garden set-up world systems that make true humility very difficult. Purposefully, he has arranged traps and snares using the thirteen "E's" of Pride. Not meant to be an exhaustive list, the thirteen "E's" of Pride are: economy, employment, entertainment, enticement, enraging, envying, erecting, enrichment, equalization, evagation, evolution, ecclesiastical and esurience. In many of these areas, Christians have succumbed and have given the "high" ground to Satan. Each "E" will be briefly explored to expose how Satan and his demons try to keep unbelievers and even disciples full of pride.

Economy

Over the last several years, many have witnessed first-hand the world's preoccupation with global economic events. Never in the history of the planet has an international financial crisis commenced from what should have been an isolated small country event. This fixation and world connectedness has created a comprehensive Ponzi scheme in which only a few global elitists will be able to withstand. Hence, the Devil has set the "economy" trap, utilizing twenty-four hour markets, pegged currencies, CNBC, the World Bank, the IMF and the United Nations. Anxiety and fear (stemming from pride) have gripped much of the populace with this first "E". Too many Christians have succumbed as well.

Employment

The next "E", employment, is just economics taken to a personal level. Over the last century, Satan has effectively engulfed the world with entanglements between evil and occupations. Many are faced with compromising their Biblically-based convictions. A few obvious examples of lawful occupations that present Christian workers with an immediate decision are: alcoholic beverage industry jobs, abortion clinic professionals, casino positions, nightclub/bar employees and anything involved with the "legal" sex trade. Sadly, "christians" have somehow rationalized working in these unbiblical industries because of wanting to "provide for their family" or "put food on the table." Some of these compromises would have been unheard of 60 years ago, but the manifestation of the pride of wanting higher paying jobs in growing industries, located near "good" school districts, is just too much to disregard. More common are the less egregious examples of compromise that exist across so-called "benign" commerce. This occurs when individual companies have taken stances against God. A too common example is found when companies decide to promote homosexuality through externally sponsored events or internally driven "diversity/sensitivity" indoctrination. A recent example comes from a well-known national retailer (Macy's) that started allowing male transvestites the use of ladies changing rooms. In all of these types of cases, saints need to pray, read God's Words, and seek the Holy Spirit's guidance in order to make God-honoring choices. In many cases, it may initially be easier to be quiet, to stay employed, and get paid. In the long run, the consequences to self, family, and in relation to God far outweigh the benefits of compromise.

Entertainment

The third "E", entertainment, is often a prideful stumbling block for believers. Here, the Christian incorrectly believes that they have "liberty" in Christ to "enjoy" lewd, profane, and God-blaspheming entertainment. Often coming from an industry which is at war with God (Hollywood), it may at first appear "benign." However, once entangled with the amusement, demonic incrementalism into deeper depravity occurs. The foolish ego makes man think that he is impervious to Satan's wiles. One must not forget that to "amuse," literally means, "not to think" and if one were not thinking, then one would not be continually "renewing the mind," as Paul admonished (Rom. 12:2).

Enticement

The next "E", enticement, is nothing less than packaging the sin in such a way that it appeals to pride through the senses. It is Satan transforming himself into an "angel of light" to appear beneficial (2 Cor. 11:14). Enticement is key to First John 2:16: *"For all that is in the world, the lust of the flesh, and the lust of the eyes, and the pride of life, is not of the Father, but is of the world."* Sin undeniably has temporal appeal or else no one would partake. But once the early charm has waned, the individual is left in bondage and often broken and destroyed.

Enraging

One of the more destructive manifestations of pride comes from the "E" of enraging. It is the antithesis of patience and temperance. The Bible has given many examples of wrath's consequences, some of which have been already explored (Cain & Ahab). Once pride is entrenched in the heart, then enraging will rear itself all too often. To Satan's delight, testimonies and relationships are destroyed for years.

Envying

Envying, the never satiated and covetous "E", is quintessential pride. Practically synonymous with self, it comes directly from the world-wide and still felt consequences of Beelzebub's envy of God. It is one of Satan's preferred modes of bringing devastation to mankind; believers included! This may be why God abhors covetousness (Psa. 10:3) and calls envy "rottenness of the bones" (Prov. 14:30). Envy is a great preventer of humility.

Erecting

The next "E", erecting, is keeping busy with the stuff of life. It's moving things from point A to point B without it having eternal value. It's just slightly above the activity of ants. Our Lord and Saviour spoke of this very thing in the "Parable of the Sower." Christ said that some will only briefly respond to the Gospel but through "erecting" and "busyness" the Word will be choked.

> *And the cares of this world, and the deceitfulness of riches, and the lusts of other things entering in, choke the word, and it becometh unfruitful. (Mark. 4:19)*

Today, too many Christians are involved in things of the world at the expense of all that is Biblical. They will work on their house and yard ten to fifteen hours per week but may give God an hour of worship and another hour of prayer and reading per week; and that's if they're diligent. Many are much worse and then wonder why their walk with God is anemic and why there hasn't really been a change in their lives since "going to church" and "buying a Bible." Only doing these two things deceives many into thinking that they will be entering God's eternal kingdom. How gravely they are mistaken, as it can be a mark of false conversion.

Enrichment

Moving to enrichment, this "E" is identified as having everything one thinks they need in life. (e.g. A beautiful four bedroom, two-and-a-half bath, two-car garage with two relatively new cars inside.) This coincides with regular vacations to Disney World or Myrtle Beach as well as owning every electronic device known to man. Some would aptly call this the Pride of Materialism. One of the more appropriate verses comes from the man that had more riches, power, women, and proverbial wisdom than any man ever. Regarding materialism, King Solomon writes,

> *"Labour not to be rich: cease from thine own wisdom. Wilt thou set thine eyes upon that which is not? for riches certainly make themselves wings; they fly away as an eagle toward heaven." (Prov. 23:4-5)*

Riches, like other Satanic devices, are merely temporal. If Satan can offer worldly kingdoms to Jesus, he can unquestionably do it on a lesser scale to human beings.

Equalization

Fittingly, next addressed is an "E" that turns 180 degrees against the "disparities" created by materialism. Equalization, through Godless Marxism and Socialism, has been used by the Devil for over 100 years to deceive believers into thinking that poverty can be eliminated and that "communitarianism" is truly the message that Christ wanted to communicate to the world. Cleverly, Satan has used this vehicle to manipulate the pride of man into thinking that making everyone financially equal will solve the world's maladies. This "E" goes hand-in-hand with grave doctrinal errors like "Post-Millennialism" and the "Social Gospel." Have believers forgotten that Christ said that we will always have the poor (Matt. 26:11; Mark 14:7; John 12:8)? Have followers neglected that the true "commune" was exclusively made up of like-minded believers? *"And all that believed were together, and had all things common; And sold their possessions and goods, and parted them to all men, as every man had need."* (Acts. 2:44-45) Through this mechanism, Satan has deceived many into discarding Biblical "re-birth" through repentance and faith in Christ alone and has succeeded in propagating heretical "works" and "process" salvation.

Evagation

The next "E", evagation, reflects the wandering and roving of man. Today some would call it "jet-setting" or moving to "climb the corporate ladder." Any way you look at it, it describes the transitory nature of man's pride. Satan has long ago tapped into this sensation. In part, this transience has naturally bred lack of accountability and lack of commitment. "Why bother being good, going to church or getting to know others if I will be moving in two years?" The book of Daniel describes part of this phenomenon:

> *But thou, O Daniel, shut up the words, and seal the book, even to the time of the end: many shall run to and fro, and knowledge shall be increased. (Dan. 12:4)*

This could also be a prelude to what Jesus Christ reveals will occur during the tribulation:

> *And because iniquity shall abound, the love of many shall wax cold. (Matt. 24:12)*

Evolution

The "E" of evolution has been mightily used by Satan to tap into the intellectual pride of man. In this "E", Satan has made great inroads at undermining several foundational truths of the Bible such as: God created all things in six literal days, God made man from His image, and the woman from the man, and sin came before death. Since it is a myth, the "Theory of Evolution" is replete with astronomical, anthropological and archeological inconsistencies. While having basic knowledge of Carbon 14 Dating, Argon Diffusion, and Radioisotope Dating is helpful, all believers should at least commit to memory the following verse:

> *Beware lest any man spoil you through philosophy and vain deceit, after the tradition of men, after the rudiments of the world, and not after Christ."(Col. 2:8)*

In the end, you need more faith to believe in evolution than to believe in God, Jesus Christ and the Bible.

Ecclesiastical

The next to last "E" is ecclesiastical. This again is one of the areas where Satan, using the temptation weapon of pride, has inflicted considerable damage to God's people. Through the use of false prophets and teachers, as well as ungodly or unqualified leaders, many unsaved have been deceived into thinking that real brethren are just as bad, if not worse, than the world. For example, man has still not seen the end of all of the sufferings that will be created through Bishop Eddie Long's pride. Even the ecclesiastical pride that comes from true saints disputing matters of theology can become an issue, as written by C.H. Spurgeon:

> Pride can be found in every rank in society, among all classes of men. Sometimes it is an Arminian, and talks of the power of the creature. Then it turns Calvinistic, and boasts of its fancied security, forgetful of the Maker who alone can keep faith alive....It attends all kinds of chapels and churches. Look where you will, you will see pride. It comes up with us to the house of God. It goes with us to our houses.[80]

Christians in non-leadership roles are not immune as it will invariably impact their fellowship with God.

Esurience

The last "E" pride comes from the rarely used word esurience. Esurience speaks of eating lavishly and luxuriously. While it all sounds very fanciful, it is nothing less than common everyday gluttony. The Devil has used the extravagance of food, drink, and other Items, to be a stumbling block for people. People, even believers, do not equate unrestrained succumbing to the flesh with pride. Christ and the Apostles often fasted as a means to draw closer to God and to provide followers with an example of godliness: *"As they ministered to the Lord, and fasted, the Holy Ghost said, Separate me Barnabas and Saul for the work whereunto I have called them. And when they had fasted and prayed, and laid their hands on them, they sent them away."* (Acts. 13:2-3)

Even though some know intellectually that it's possible to achieve humility, many have given up the quest, partly due to their repeated failures. With that as background, it is finally the moment to explore how to attain

---

[80] Charles Haddon Spurgeon.
http://www.Spurgeon.us/mind_and_heart/quotes/p4.htm#pride (accessed October 3, 2011)

and retain Christ-centered humility in our lives while combating the aforementioned snares and traps of Satan.

CHAPTER 20

HOW TO ATTAIN AND RETAIN CHRIST-CENTERED HUMILITY

The Presence of God is Necessary

As examined earlier, it will not be easy to exhibit Christ-like humility and meekness. True humility will not come on its own. It must be the object of fervent prayer, faith, and practice. One must desire this virtue. But one thing is certain; only the presence of God can reveal and expel pride, and ultimately replace it with humility. Only He can help accept every humiliation. Only He can help one look upon those that irritate as a means to gracefully humble. But how does one get to that point?

The First Step For the Believer: Prayer

For the believer, the first step is to ask God, in prayer, to reveal the pride in his heart and how it manifests itself. *This is critical because the more undetectable pride is, the more damage it inflicts on the possessor and those in vicinity*. In parallel, one must identify personal areas that have not been submitted to God. These areas of sin bondage initially grew from pride and are equally sustained by it. Likewise, this sin bondage will prevent true humility from taking residence in the heart. It effectively blots out the Holy Spirit's conviction and weakens the power of prayers and petitions.

Return to the Teaching of the Bible

One next must return to the teachings of the Lamb of God, Jesus Christ. Here is what He said about being one of His disciples:

> *Then said Jesus unto his disciples, If any man will come after me, let him deny himself, and take up his cross, and follow me. (Matt. 16:24)*

It is foundational that one has to deny himself, his fleshly wants and worldly desires. One must follow Christ in his mind:

> *Serving the LORD with all humility of mind, and with many tears, and temptations, which befell me by the lying in wait of the Jews. (Acts 20:19)*

It also implies doing what He would have done while accepting with gratitude everything that God allows as a reminder for the need of humbling. It is here when a believer begins to earnestly crave humility in his life.

Thirteen Biblical Steps Toward Humility

Offered below are Biblically-based steps towards achieving and maintaining humility.

1. Realize that pride is present in my life.
2. Ask God to forgive me for being prideful.
3. Pray that God will give me the ability to turn from pride and to set a daily hedge of protection.
4. Remember where I came from and how far God has brought me since salvation and all of His provision.
5. Read, meditate and memorize Scriptures daily (Luke 9:23; Gal. 2:20-21; 1 Cor. 15:31).
6. Ask God to help me stop comparing myself to others.
7. Serve in local church ministries as God directs
8. Seek fellowship and accountability with believers.
9. Be willing to experience adversity and/or every humiliation. Anything that drives me to God is always good for me.
10. Understand that mankind deserves to experience God's judgment and wrath because of sin (Eph. 2:3).
11. Meditate about the "Day of Judgment" where every evil thought, desire, word and action will be judged (2 Cor. 5:10; Rev. 20:12).
12. If a believer, turn every area of your life over to Christ.
13. Worship God at every possible opportunity.

Surrender Prideful Habits

Brethren should also take the opportunity to become lower anytime they read, sing, or act out something that is closer to God than they presently are living. If this occurs, the lowly must ask God for forgiveness for building-up areas around the idol of self. For it to succeed, a person must exhibit true repentance and immediately surrender these prideful habits to God.

Finally, one should be thankful to God for all circumstances as they are an opportunity to draw nigh to God.

> "Whatever God gives thee be grateful for, for if too proud to take from the raven's mouth, it will be well for thee to go without, until thine hunger consume thy pride."[81]

How often should the born-again live out the above recommendations? The answer is daily!

> "We all need to remember and reflect upon this idea of humility every day of our lives."[82]

Our prayer should be to be humbled daily unto Christ's death. A daily death to self!

> "Enter, in His grave, into rest from self and its work – the rest of God. With Christ, who committed His spirit into the Father's hands, humble yourself and descend each day into that perfect, helpless dependence on God. God will raise you up and exalt you."[83]

---

[81] Charles Haddon Spurgeon. www.finestquotes.com. http://www.finestquotes.com/author_quotes-author Charles%20H.%20Spurgeon-page-0.htm (accessed January 8, 2011)

[82] Tony Dungy, <u>Uncommon</u> (Carol Stream, IL: Tyndale House, 2009), 25.

[83] Andrew Murray, <u>Humility</u> (New Kensington, PA: Whitaker, 1982), 96.

Never Forget These Three Promises

Christians should never forget the following three New Testament promises for faithful and loving believers of God:

> *Now unto him that is able to do exceeding abundantly above all that we ask or think, according to the power that worketh in us. (Eph. 3:20);*

> *And we know that all things work together for good to them that love God, to them who are the called according to his purpose. (Rom. 8:28);*

> *Jesus said unto him, If thou canst believe, all things are possible to him that believeth. (Mark 9:23).*

God is saying that humility and meekness are more than possible, they are a certainty. The Bible makes it clear that Christians are responsible; they just have to do their part.

CHAPTER 21

HOW TO DEAL WITH
THE PRIDE OF OTHERS

Perceived Rights

Only a truly humble individual will be able to effectively deal with a haughty individual. Otherwise, you would have two people who are solely concerned with their perceived rights, needs, and overall well-being. No one will be able to take the "high-road." The customary result is anger, wrath, and flight. Relationships are severed. Marriages start to crumble and eventually end up dysfunctional or in divorce. This is why the book of Proverbs states:

> *Only by pride cometh contention: but with the well advised is wisdom. (13:10)*

Strife and Defusing It

It is truly "eye-opening" to note that only evil pride causes arguments and strife. Unlike "modern" counseling, strife is not caused by not having enough money or having an insensitive or untidy spouse. Dissension is not even caused by destructive adultery or lack of affection; it is caused solely by self-love and arrogance. The other sins are merely the secondary cause but not the root. It is interesting to observe that if one of the two parties possesses humility, any dissension and/or discord is summarily eliminated. Why? Because the proud person has no one to fiercely combat. It becomes a "one-sided" engagement, as it is no longer a "fight" but purely a monologue. Typically, the arguer runs out of things to say when no one is responding. There is no additional fuel or oxygen for the fire. This is another confirmation why believers should tightly embrace the Biblical truth of James 1:19:

> *Wherefore, my beloved brethren, let every man be swift to hear, slow to speak, slow to wrath.*

Factors to Consider

The humble believer must also take into account several factors as he deals with a proud counterpart. The first, and most important, consideration is the depth (or lack thereof) of the proud person's "walk" with Christ. For the most part, an unsaved person should be handled differently than someone who is a "baby" Christian. Conversely, a "baby" Christian should be treated differently than a mature saint. A mature believer should always be looking to impart the Gospel of salvation to an unsaved person and should be focused on correctly discipling an immature believer.

One must next consider how the sinful pride is manifesting itself. Someone who is a proud workaholic will be addressed differently than someone who is a proud sloth. Someone who is proudly well-dressed (suit and tie) will be ministered to differently than someone who is shabbily dressed (tattered jeans) or someone who is moderately dressed (Khakis and golf shirt) and proud of it. All three can reveal the chameleon-like nature of pride since all may be feeling loftier and grander in comparison to others. Other important factors such as age, sex, and specific traumas should also be prayed about and deliberated.

Seek the Guidance of the Holy Spirit

In the end, the regenerated Bible-believing individual must seek the guidance of the Holy Spirit in dealing with proud people. Prayer, meditation, and fasting must also be part of seeking the Lord's will in this matter. One must not lose sight of the fact that demonic influences are at play in this interaction. The likelihood of this situation being satanically produced in order to create a trap for the believer is very real. Paul writes of this to Timothy:

> *In meekness instructing those that oppose themselves; if God peradventure will give them repentance to the acknowledging of the truth; And that they may recover*

themselves out of the snare of the devil, who are taken captive by him at his will. (2 Tim. 2:25-26)

The Desired Goal

The desired end-result of interacting with a proud unbeliever is to bring him/her to earnest Biblical contrition and repentance. Repentance can then pave the way for heart-belief in the resurrection and deity of Jesus Christ; a miraculous conversion. For the immature believer, the wanted result is conviction and a drawing closer to Jesus Christ - ideally creating in him a renewed mind and a sense that worldly things are foolishness to Christ. *"Let no man deceive himself. If any man among you seemeth to be wise in this world, let him become a fool, that he may be wise."* (1 Cor. 3:18) Most significantly, the proven saint should strive to impart the "young" believer with the zeal to serve God and to reach those that are in darkness, as they were not long before.

Conclusion

After accepting Jesus Christ, "The highest lesson a believer has to learn is humility."[84] This is so because so much of the growth in Christ comes from a desire to humble ourselves to God and Jesus Christ. All one has, and is, comes from God. It is only when one is truly humble that he can have closeness with Jesus Christ in his daily walk. His prayers then have power. The Holy Spirit's continuous presence is felt. It is when a disciple is most protected and when earthly and heavenly blessings will be most experienced.

It stands to reason that all should not concentrate just on learning about humility, but start living it out as it pleases God. As stated earlier, one should absolutely focus on reading and meditating on God's word. But beyond reading and meditating, one should strive to apply humility, meekness, lowliness, gentleness, modesty and abasement in the daily walk. God and His words state that saints will be blessed for it. It's either "...Being humble or being humbled."[85]

Finally, why should believers spend time understanding humility and applying it in life? The response is simply because humility is key and necessary to faith, repentance, and acceptance of Jesus Christ as Lord and Savior, and as such, provides a living testimony to a world lying in darkness. *"What is then, or in what lies, the great struggle for eternal life? It lies entirely in the battle between pride and humility."*[86]

One question one must forthrightly ask is, "Who is going to be the final authority in my life"? Will it be Satan, the created being whose heinous pride has helped produce

---

[84] Andrew Murray, <u>Humility</u> (New Kensington, PA: Whitaker, 1982), 101.

[85] Charles Haddon Spurgeon. www.spurgeon.us. http://www.spurgeon.us/mind_and_heart/quotes /h2 htm#humility (accessed January 8, 2011).

[86] Andrew Murray, <u>Humility</u> (New Kensington, PA: Whitaker, 1982), 118.

counterfeit "religions" to confuse the undiscerning? He who wants you to be in bondage to despair and wants to separate you eternally from the Creator Father God in a fiery place of torment and gnashing of teeth. Will it be Jesus Christ, the meek and humble Lamb of God who does not want anyone to perish but all to come to repentance and have everlasting life through Him? The Eternal One who desires to bestow eternal blessings upon His followers, and who wants those that believe in Him to live eternally with Him and God the Father. The choice should be absolutely clear. There can be no middle ground. *"Ye cannot drink the cup of the Lord, and the cup of devils: ye cannot be partakers of the Lord's table, and of the table of devils."* (1 Cor. 10:21)

We must not forget that all of the thanks and glory goes to Almighty God!

> *Giving thanks unto the Father, which hath made us meet to be partakers of the inheritance of the saints in light: Who hath delivered us from the power of darkness, and hath translated us into the kingdom of his dear Son. (Col. 1:12-13)*

> *Whether therefore ye eat, or drink, or whatsoever ye do, do all to the glory of God. (1 Cor. 10:31)*

While the glory and thanks goes to God the Father, we do all in the Name of His Son: Our Saviour and Lord Jesus Christ:

> *And whatsoever ye do in word or deed, do all in the name of the Lord Jesus, giving thanks to God and the Father by him. (Col. 3:17)*

Even so, come, Lord Jesus. Amen.

BIBLIOGRAPHY

Holy Bible: The Authorized King James Version. New York: Oxford, 1945.

Bounds, Edward McKendree. The Complete Works of E.M. Bounds (Baker Books 1990)

Dungy, Tony. Uncommon (Carol Stream, IL: Tyndale House Publishers 2009)

Fenton, Gary. Good for Goodness' Sake: 7 Values for Cultivating Authentic Character in Midlife (Birmingham, AL: New Hope Publishing 2006)

Haines, Erin. "Megachurch's Future Uncertain after Pastor Leaves" Associated Press. December 5, 2011

Jensen, Sean. "Jason Wright passes up NFL contract to attend business school" Yahoo! Sports. September 20, 2011

Kempis, Thomas A. The Imitation of Christ (Netherlands, Public Domain, 1418)

Logan, Jim. Reclaiming Surrendered Ground (Chicago, IL: Moody Press 1995)

MacArthur, John. The Murder of Jesus (Nashville, TN: Word Publishing 2000)

MacArthur, John. The MacArthur New Testament Commentary (Nashville, TN: Thomas Nelson 2007)

Mack, Wayne. Humility: The Forgotten Virtue (Phillipsburg, NJ: P&R Publishing 2005)

McQuilkin, Robertson. Understanding and Applying the Bible (Chicago, IL: Moody Publishers 1992)

Murray, Andrew. Humility (New Kensington, PA: Whitaker House 1982)

Palmer, Kimberly. "The Secret to Living Well on $40,000 a Yearl". <u>U.S. News and World Report</u>. September 23, 201.

Poole, Shelia M. "Eddie Long case officially dismissed". <u>The Atlanta Journal-Constitution.</u> May 27, 2011

Robinson, Eugene. "Pride Goeth Before the Headlines." <u>Ebony Magazine</u>. December/November 2011

Scott, Stuart. <u>From Pride to Humility: A Biblical Perspective</u> (Bemidji, MN: Focus Publishing Incorporated 2010)

Stanley, Charles. <u>Landmines in the Path of the Believer</u> (Nashville, TN: Thomas Nelson 2007)

Stowell, Joseph M. <u>Tongue in Check</u> (Wheaton, IL: Victor Books 1983)

Strong, James. <u>Strong's Talking Greek & Hebrew Dictionary</u> (Austin, TX: WORDsearch Corp., 2007)

Wiersbe, Warren. <u>The Strategy of Satan</u> (Carol Stream, IL: Tyndale House Publishers 1979)

www.brainyquote.com

www.finestquotes.com

www.thefreedictionary.com
www.spurgeon.us

www.webster-dictionary.org

SCRIPTURE CITINGS

1. **Genesis** - 1:26-27; 2:16-17; 3:1, 4-8, 12-19; 4:4, 7-9; 6:5, 12; 9:1, 6; 11:4-5, 9; 18:2; 23:7-12; 33:3-7; 37:2, 13; 39:21; 42:24; 43:30; 45:2, 14-15; 46:29; 48:12; 50:17.
2. **Exodus** – 2:21-22; 3:2-4:21; 6:30; 10:3; 15:25; 18:1-27; 40:16.
3. **Leviticus** – 26:19-20, 41.
4. **Numbers** – 12:3; 14:1-4, 11; 15:30-31; 16:28; 22:22-35; 25:2.
5. **Deuteronomy** – 6:10-12; 8:2-3, 16; 22:24-29; 28:43; 32:4; 34:7.
6. **Joshua** – 5:6; 23:16.
7. **Judges** – 2:17; 11:35; 19:24.
8. **Ruth** – 2:10.
9. **I Samuel** – 1:6-7; 11; 2:1-3, 5-10; 13:14; 16:11, 23; 17:15, 20, 28-29, 45-47, 58; 18:5, 23; 20:41; 24:8; 28:14; 30:4.
10. **II Samuel** – 1:11-12; 6:16; 12:1-14, 22; 13:31; 22:28; 24:15.
11. **I Kings** – 2:2-4; 3:9, 12-14; 4:32; 11:1-3, 5-8; 12:8, 13-14; 14:22-24; 16:29; 18:18; 19:18; 20:7, 14, 42; 19:2; 21:25, 29; 22:5-8, 19, 39, 46.
12. **II Kings** – 5:12; 9:30; 18:3; 21:2, 11-12; 22:2, 19; 23:22, 25.
13. **I Chronicles** - 28:9; 29:20.
14. **II Chronicles** – 2:7, 12, 14; 7:3, 14; 11:4, 21; 12:1, 5-7, 12; 19:2; 20:3, 18, 37; 25:14; 26:5, 16, 18-21; 28:19; 30:11; 32:26; 33:9, 12-13, 15-16, 23-34; 34:27; 35:18; 36:17-21.
15. **Nehemiah** – 8:6; 9:16, 29.
16. **Esther** – 3:1-6, 8-9, 13, 15; 5:11-13.
17. **Job** – 1:1, 21-22; 2:10; 9:13; 22:29; 32:1; 33:17; 35:12; 38:4; 40:11, 12; 42:2-6.
18. **Psalms** – 5:9; 9:12; 10:2-4, 10, 17; 12:6-7; 17:10; 19:66; 22:26; 25:9; 31:18-20; 34:2-3, 12, 18; 35:13-14; 36:2, 4; 37:11; 38:6; 40:4; 44:8, 21; 49:6-9; 51:1-6, 17; 57:6; 59:12; 69:10, 32; 73:6-11; 76:9; 86:14; 94:4; 97:7; 101:5; 106:43; 107:29; 116:6, 12-19; 119:21, 51, 66, 69, 78, 85, 122; 123:4; 136:23; 138:6; 140:5, 8; 142:6; 145:17; 146:8; 147:6; 149:4.
19. **Proverbs** - 6:3, 17; 8:13; 9:8; 10:19; 11:2, 4, 13; 12:23; 13:1, 10; 14:9, 30; 15:13, 25, 33; 16:5, 18, 19; 18:1, 11, 12; 19:20; 20:12; 21:4, 24; 22:4, 6; 23:4-5; 25:14; 26:12, 16; 27:1, 2, 5-6; 28:2, 11, 13, 25; 29:5, 23.
20. **Ecclesiastes** – 5:13; 7:8; 12:4, 8, 13-14.
21. **Isaiah** – 2:9, 11, 17; 3:1, 5, 16-17; 5:14, 15, 20-21; 6:5; 9:6, 9-12; 10:15, 33; 11:4; 13:11; 14:11-14; 16:6; 20:3; 24:4; 25:5, 11; 26:5; 28:1-3; 29:4, 19; 38:1; 53:7; 57:15; 61:1, 6; 66:2.
22. **Jeremiah** – 3:9; 13:9, 15, 17-18; 17:9; 43:2; 44:10; 48:29; 49:16; 50:29-32; 51:20-23.

23. **Lamentations** – 3:19-20.
24. **Ezekiel** – 16:48-50, 56; 21:26; 22:10-11; 28:11-19; 30:6.
25. **Daniel** – 1:3-5, 8, 19-21; 2:15, 20-24, 26-45, 47, 49; 3:15, 19, 21-27; 4:3, 27, 30, 37; 5:17, 20; 6:5, 21, 22; 9:2; 12:4, 8, 9-10.
26. **Hosea** – 5:5; 7:9-11; 13:6.
27. **Obadiah** – 1:3.
28. **Habakkuk** - 2:5.
29. **Zephaniah** - 2:3, 9-11; 3:11.
30. **Zechariah** – 9:6, 9; 10:11.
31. **Malachi** – 3:15; 4:1.
32. **Matthew** – 1:19, 24-25; 2:13-14, 20-21; 4:19-20; 5:3-5, 7, 39; 6:22-23; 7:3-5; 15; 8:8-10, 12; 9:10-11; 10:16, 37; 11:19, 28-30; 12:31, 34, 37, 47; 13:42; 15:27-28; 16:6, 18, 24; 17:25; 18:3-4, 17, 22, 28-30; 19:18; 20:10-12, 26-28; 21:31-32; 22:13, 18, 37-40; 23:11, 12, 24-28, 33; 24:12, 51; 25:46; 26:11, 40, 75; 27:29.
33. **Mark** – 2:15-16; 3:29, 31; 7:2, 6, 21-23; 8:33; 9:19, 23, 42; 10:11-12, 19, 24, 43-45; 11:7; 12:36-37; 14:7, 37; 15:40.
34. **Luke** - 1:38, 46-55; 3:12-13; 5:8, 29-32; 6:29; 7:34; 8:19; 9:41, 48; 11:39; 12:51-53; 13:3, 15, 28; 14:11, 26; 15:11; 16:19-31; 17:2; 18:9-14, 20; 19:2-11; 22:26, 27; 23:48; 24:5, 12.
35. **John** - 1:1-3, 12; 2:4, 5, 12; 4:34; 6:38-40, 68-69; 7:16, 34; 8:28, 29, 50; 9:34; 10:18-19; 13; 12:8, 25; 13:9, 14, 38; 16:22-23; 17:1-5; 18:15; 19:25-27; 21:7, 17, 20-22, 25.
36. **Acts** – 1:14-15; 2:1, 14-41, 44-45; 3:6, 12; 4:19; 5:3, 5, 29; 7:22, 36; 8:20; 9:34, 39-41; 10:26, 44, 48; 13:2-3, 22; 15:7-11; 20:9, 18, 19, 31-38; 26:5.
37. **Romans** - 1:25-27, 29-31; 5:3; 6:12; 7:18; 8:14, 27, 28, 29; 9:19-23; 10:9-10; 11:4, 20-21; 12:2, 3, 6, 10, 15, 16; 13:1-2; 14:10.
38. **I Corinthians** – 1:10-13, 31; 2:14; 3:3, 18, 19; 4:7, 21; 5:2, 6; 6:19-20; 7:5; 8:1, 9; 9:24-25; 10:21, 31; 13:4; 15:9; 16:7, 8.
39. **II Corinthians** – 2:11; 4:4; 5:7, 10, 12, 14-15; 6:14-15; 7:14; 9:2; 10:1, 8, 13, 17; 11:14-15; 12:7-10, 20.
40. **Galatians** - 1:10; 2:11-14; 5:13, 22-23; 6:1, 2, 3.
41. **Ephesians** - 2:2, 3, 9; 3:8, 20; 4:2, 3, 15, 29; 5:21, 22; 6:6.
42. **Philippians** – 1:21; 2:3-4, 6-8, 21; 3:12-14; 4:6-7, 12.
43. **Colossians** – 1:12-13; 2:8; 18, 23; 3:10, 12-14, 17, 22.
44. **I Thessalonians** – 2:18-20; 3:5; 4:13-18; 5:17, 18.
45. **I Timothy** – 1:15; 2:1-2; 3:6, 15; 4:1-2, 7-9; 6:1-5, 9-10, 17-18.
46. **II Timothy** – 2:1-2, 25-26; 3:1-6, 8, 9; 4:6-8.
47. **Titus** – 3:2.
48. **Hebrews** – 1:10; 6:3; 10:25; 11:24-25; 12:2.
49. **James** - 1:1, 9, 12, 19, 21; 2:18-20; 3:2, 5-6, 13; 4:6, 7, 10, 14; 5:11.
50. **I Peter** – 2:13-17; 3:1, 3, 4, 5, 10-11, 15; 5:2-6, 8.

51. **II Peter** – 1:5-8; 2:1, 5, 18, 19; 3:18.
52. **I John** – 1:9-10; 2:15-17; 3:1, 2; 4:20.
53. **III John** – 1:9-11.
54. **Jude** – 1:16
55. **Revelation** - 2:10, 23; 3:10; 4:9-10; 16:14; 20:11-15; 22:15.

208

INDEX

Printed in the USA
CPSIA information can be obtained
at www.ICGtesting.com
CBHW060313091024
15401CB00008BA/101